Acting is Acting

Your Step by Step Acting Guidebook

Lovena Kureemun

Kureemun Books Ltd

London

Copyright

An imprint of Kureemun Books Ltd

London

Table of Content

Chapter 5- Working with the lines

5.1) Inner images for your lines
    5.1.1) Definition of inner images
    5.1.2) How to create inner images?

5.2) Inner images for your scene partner's lines

5.3) Inner monologues for your scene partner's lines
    5.3.1) Definition of inner monologues
    5.3.2) Finding inner monologue for your scene partner's lines

5.4) Your beat changes
    5.4.1) Definition of beat changes

5.5) Action words / action verbs

5.6) Connecting the lines of the script
    5.6.1) How do you connect each line?
    5.6.2) What is improvisation?

Recap of Working with the lines

Chapter 6 - Rehearsals

6.1) Let go of the preparations you have done so far

6.2) Finding the subtext between you and your scene partner
    6.2.1) Meeting with your scene partner
    6.2.2) What is the subtext between you and your scene partner?
    6.2.3) How to find the subtext between you and your scene partner?
    6.2.4) Finding the subtext between you and your scene partner to rehearse a monologue.

6.3) Rehearsing with your scene partner
    6.3.1) Listening, talking, and responding
    6.3.2) Moment to moment acting

6.4) First rehearsal

6.5) Second rehearsal

6.6) Third rehearsal

6.7) Rehearsing a monologue

Dedication

To my brother, Harishen and mother, Lata Devi

Introduction

Acting is Acting is a step by step guidebook designed to guide you when you have to work on a new script and prepare a scene/ monologue for an audition.

A script is a problem that actors use their imagination, creativity, mind, body and soul to solve in order to create a great character that will serve the story of the script.

There are two main parts that contribute to a great acting performance:

Part One: Working off your scene partner
- You are alive with your imagination, thoughts, emotions, feelings, fears and desires.
- You are in the moment of talking, listening and responding truthfully.
- You are allowing each moment to build up as you go.
- You are observing, perceiving your partner and maintaining a soul to soul connection with your scene partner.
- You are being affected by a number of stimuli and express your responses to those stimuli in a creative way.
- You are being instinctive, impulsive and intuitive.

Part Two: Working from the facts of the script
- You are acting the imaginary circumstances and the dramatic event of the story.

Thus, in order to fulfil the above two main parts, every actor has to go through seven steps. And this book, Acting is Acting, focuses on those seven steps on how to guide you to give a great performance.

The seven steps that any actor goes through while working on a new script are:

1. **Freeing the obstacle of an actor** - To understand how to eliminate all your obstacles as an actor, thus to allow you to be free, to know the essence of your true self and express that truthfully.
2. **Reading the script** - To familiarize yourself with the story of the scene or the play or the monologue and to guide you on how to read a script for the first time and 100th time.
3. **Scene analysis** -To identify the characters, the dramatic event, the relationships, the time, the place, the props, the activities, the overall sensations, the Moment Before and the arc of the character which are the ten imaginary circumstances of a scene.
4. **Scene analysis into practice**- To guide you in identifying choices through personalization, substitutions and use of sense memory, hence to support you to bring yourself to the imaginary circumstances of the scene. Consequently, this will help you to act the imaginary circumstances and the dramatic event of the scene.
5. **Working with the lines** - To help you in creating and identifying inner images, inner monologues and beat changes according the lines of the script. Also, to help you in connecting the lines of the script together.
6. **Rehearsals** - To guide you to work off your scene partner and to make choices off what the scene partner is giving back to you while rehearsing the scene

7. **Performance Day** - To prepare yourself during the performance day of your scene

Chapter 1- Freeing obstacles of an actor

Freeing obstacles of an actor is the process of finding the actors' true self and of guiding them to express the true self impulsively, instinctively and intuitively through their actions, behaviors, speeches and movements.

In this chapter, you will learn the following:
1) How does a human being function?
2) The obstacles of an actor
3) Exercises to free the obstacles of an actor
4) Other activities

1.1) How does a human being function?

You are a human being before an actor, you are a human being with thoughts, feelings, emotions, desires, wants, needs, ego, fears, imaginations, creativity, talents, flaws, passions, dreams, goals and many more qualities with individual characteristics.

Acting is life and life is acting. To understand acting, you should understand how a human being function.

Human beings' function by the use of the followings:
1) Their mind
2) Their body
3) Their soul

1.1.1 The mind

The Mind of a human being has four main functions: **The conscious mind, the intellectual mind, the subconscious mind and the ego.**

The Conscious mind
The conscious mind allows human beings to interact with the external world using their five senses (sight, touch, smell, taste and sound). Human beings process sensory information collected though sight, touch, sound and smell in their mind. The conscious mind is the waking state of the mind which makes human beings aware of the present.

The intellectual mind
The intellectual mind allows human beings to think, plan, decide, judge and analyze. It controls the thoughts, feelings, emotions and the will of human beings. The intellectual mind prevents human

beings from express their true self, true feelings, true emotions and true instincts.

The subconscious mind
The subconscious mind is the storage of human beings' experiences. The subconscious mind is the location where human beings' wild dreams, imaginations and creative ideas originate from.

The ego
The ego creates identity of the self of human beings and creates the "I AM".

1.1.2) The soul

The soul is the essence of the true self of human beings. The soul is where human beings' instincts, inner voices, intuitions, impulses, and involuntary movements come from. **It is where the truth of human beings lies.** It is the spiritual self. It is the reservoir of feelings, thoughts, desires, needs, wants and urges that is beyond the control of human beings.

1.1.3) The physical body

The physical body of human beings expresses their mind through actions, speeches, behaviors, feelings and emotions and movements.

In acting, actors' function in a similar manner by the use of their mind, body and soul. Actors express **their mind** (which is their creativity and imagination) and **their inner self** (which is their soul) using **their physical body** through speeches, actions, movement, behaviors, feelings and emotions truthfully.

1.2) The obstacles of an actor

Most actors are very sensitive and vulnerable. They get easily affected by everything that surround them. However, due to social conditionings, they have never really expressed their true self and their individuality. Consequently, most of them experience difficulties to express their emotions, actions, feelings, speeches and behaviors freely.

Factors that prevent most actors from expressing their true selves:
- Excessive thoughts what others will think about me
- Worries of not fitting in
- Thinking you are not good enough
- Worries of not being able to meet up to people's expectations and standards
- Negative thoughts
- Living in the past
- Bullied for being different and unique
- Being stuck in your intellectual mind
- Fear of rejection
- Fear of looking foolish or weird or silly
- Low self - esteem
- Lack of confidence
- Not trusting your own talents enough

The above factors have led most actors to follow a direction where they never follow their true feelings, instincts and impulses.

Hence, the goal these actors is to eliminate all these obstacles so that they can behave, act and speak as if no one is watching them. **It should be noted that to be a good actor, one should behave private in public.**

1.3) Exercises to free the obstacles of an actor

You can eliminate those obstacles by maintaining a daily routine and following some exercises which will help you to open and express your truth more often.

The list of exercises that you can follow are:
1) Breathing awareness
2) Breathing using your whole body
3) Diaphragm breathing
4) Survey of the body
5) Relaxation
6) Affirmations

Four key factors to remember while doing all those five exercises:

1. To observe what is happening with yourself and to get in touch with yourself (your moment to moment impulses, thoughts, emotions, feelings, tensions, worries and ideas).
2. To accept that those thoughts and impulses are there in you.
3. To question yourself why those thoughts and impulses are there.
4. To express those thoughts and impulses through sounds such as "HAAA" or "HUMM (Ensure the sound is fully supported by breath and coming out from your belly). You can also move, talk and express your feelings.

For example: *If you have a thought or impulse, you can express that impulse using the sound "HA HA HA" and get that impulse out of you.*

Note:
As an actor, you have to get used to express any impulse you have in the moment.

1.3.1) Breathing awareness

Breathing is the essence of life. Human beings breathe in and out unconsciously because they need air in their body to fuel them with energy to stay alive. Breath connects our body with our conscious mind.

In acting, you have to be conscious and present in the moment right now and not live in the past or worry about the future. Thus, by being aware of your breath, you will be consciously present right now in the moment.

How do we breathe?
1) We technically breathe in air through our nostrils (sometimes through our mouth), to fill in our lungs and belly.
2) Then, we breathe out air from our belly → lungs → chest → throat → then out through nostrils,
3) then we breathe in again.
4) This is how we breathe unconsciously every day.

How to do breathing awareness?
1. Be aware of your breath.
2. Place your awareness to your breath.
3. Observe how the breath enters through your nostrils.

4. Do not change the pattern.
5. Notice that there is a 1 to 3 seconds pause.
6. The breath then leaves you without even (you) forcing it.
7. There is another a 1 to 3 seconds pause.
8. The next breath then re-enters you without (you) forcing it.

1.3.2) Breathing using your whole body

As previously mentioned, we technically breathe in and out through our nostrils or through our mouth. However, for a moment, try to imagine you are breathing in from the top of your head. The breath is going down inside each part of your body (your face, arms, fingers, chest, belly, hips, legs and toes) and you are then breathing out again from your head.

How to breathe with your whole body?
1. Bring your awareness to your breathing.
2. Breathe in from the top of your head.
3. Allow the breath to travel into each part of your body (your face, arms, fingers, chest, belly, hips, legs and toes).
4. Allow the breath to leave out your body from your head at its own pace.
5. Allow the breath to come inside your body again from the top of your head.
6. **Observe, accept, understand and express any feelings, emotions, thoughts and sounds.**
7. Repeat the above 4 to 8 times daily.

1.3.3) Diaphragmatic breathing

Your diaphragm is the large horizontal oval shape muscle that is located below your lungs. When you breathe in, the diaphragm muscle moves down and when you breathe out the diaphragm muscle moves up.

The center point of the diaphragm is known as the solar plexus. The solar plexus is the center of your willpower. It is the energy center in your body which controls your confidence and your guts. It fuels you with energy to go and perform your actions in life.

Diaphragmatic breathing is essential in acting. When you concentrate on it, you will acquire the guts to express your creativity, imaginations, vulnerability and sensitivity in front of a group of people.

How to do diaphragmatic breathing?

Before doing the diaphragmatic breathing:
1. Put your focus and attention at the center of your solar plexus which is your middle point of your diaphragm.
2. Use your imagination (your mind's eyes) to picture the solar plexus in middle of your body.
3. Either close your eyes if it makes you to concentrate deeply or keep your eyes open if you are more comfortable in doing so (either way it is fine).
4. Try to keep your shoulder and upper chest still.

Doing the diaphragmatic breathing:
1. Breathe in and fill air in your belly in four directions (front of your belly, two sides of your belly and back of your belly).
2. Then fill your chest with air.
3. Pause 1 to 2 seconds consciously, count 1,2,3,4 and then breathe out.

4. Pause again 1 to 2 seconds, count 1,2,3,4 and then breathe in again.
5. Repeat the above 4-6 times daily.

1.3.4) Survey of your body

Your body is the instrument you used to express yourself. It is very common to forget the importance of the different muscles of the body. By performing the survey of your body, you will be aware of each muscle of your body.

How to do survey of your body?
1. Place your awareness on top of your head; move your attention to your facial muscles, your forehead, your eyes, your eyelids, your cheeks, your ears, your nose, your mouth, your lips, your jaw, your neck, your shoulders, your chest, your back, your arms, your elbows, your fingers, your fingertips, your abdomen, your pelvic floor, your buttocks, your hips, your knee, your ankles and your toes.
2. Focus and concentrate on each muscle; observe the subtle movements and tensions in those muscles.
3. Repeat the above exercise for 5 to 10 minutes daily.

1.3.5) Relaxation

Relaxation is about eliminating any physical tension in your body. As mentioned previously, actors use their physical body to express themselves. If the body is filled with physical tension, actors will not be able to express themselves freely. Thus, relaxation of the body is very important.

Four key factors to remember when performing relaxation:

1. To observe, accept, question and express through sounds (HA, HA, HA) on how you are feeling and sensing in the moment.
2. To continue with your breathing awareness
3. To bring your attention to each muscle of your body.
4. To focus and concentrate on the tensed muscles of your body. When you focus on the tensed area, the tension will dissipate on itself.

You have to be in control of what is happening within your body. Thus, you have to communicate with the muscles of your body and concentrate on them.

How to perform relaxation?
1. Start by tensing your facial muscles and release them out.
2. Roll your shoulders up and down; check if you have tight spots in you those area, release them.
3. Roll your head into circles by moving it left to right; if you feel any tightness in your neck area, release those tensions.
4. Lift your arms to the sides from your shoulders to your finger; move your arms, elbows and fingers in circular motion; identify any tensions and release the tensions by dropping your arms.
5. Shift your awareness to your belly; move your belly in circular motion and release any tension in that area.
6. Tense your buttocks and release the tensions.
7. Lift your legs from hips to toe and move it in small circular motions to check for any tensions; release the tensions by dropping your legs.
8. Repeat the above exercise for 10 to 20 mins daily until you feel each tension within your body has been released.

Tips:
It is recommended to read the books below:
1. **"Freeing the Natural Voice", by Kristin Linklater**
This book covers breathing, vocal and muscle exercises that are beneficial to free your obstacles as an actor.
2. **"Freeing the Actor: An Actor's Desk Reference. Over 140 Exercises and Techniques to Free the Actor", by Eric Morris**
This book contains several exercises on how to free your obstacles as an actor.

1.3.6) Affirmations

Affirmations are statements that you tell yourself to remind you who you are.

If you have negative thoughts about yourself every day and try to live up to people's expectations, you will end up believing that you are not talented and you do not have the qualities and skills to do what you want to do.

Thus, you have to rewire your subconscious mind, by filling it with positive thoughts about yourself. These positive thoughts will boost your confidence to overcome the obstacles preventing you from expressing yourself fully.

List of affirmations:
- I am confident
- I am creative
- I am imaginative
- I believe in myself

- I believe in my talents
- I am unique and different
- I am gifted
- I am courageous
- I am fearless
- I am positive
- I love myself
- I follow my impulses
- I communicate my feelings
- I express my real self freely
- I express my creativity and imagination freely.
- I trust my instincts
- I am creative
- I speak my truth clearly
- I follow my instincts
- I feel safe and secure
- I am wanted and accepted everywhere
- I do not care what others say about me
- I am free
- I am daring
- I take risks
- I am proud to be different and unique

Note:
These are NOT the only set of affirmations; you can create your own based on your true qualities and by being positive about yourself and love yourself.

1.4) Other activities

The purpose of the above exercises is to eliminate the obstacle in order to express yourself freely and to be in the moment. However, these exercises might be uninteresting or boring over time. You can bring fun to it by being involved in activities you love to do, for instance:

1) Physical activities - sports, running, spinning or rowing and boxing
2) Meditation
3) Yoga
4) Singing
5) Dancing
6) Creative activities, such as writing, drawing, and painting.

Please note before performing the exercises, it is advised you consult a medical practitioner if you have or suffer from any breathing or health related conditions.

Chapter 2-Reading the script

Reading the script is about how you would read a new play or a scene or a monologue.

In this chapter you will learn the following:
1. What is a script and a play?
2. What is a scene and a monologue?
3. Reading the script
4. First time reading the script
5. 100th time reading the script

2.1) What is a script and a play?

A script
A script is a written text of a play or a movie.

A play or a movie
A play or a movie is a story which involves a series of scenes. These scenes consist of characters and dialogues which capture the present life circumstances of people and the obstacles they face.

2.2) What is a scene and a monologue?

A scene
A scene is a dramatic event happening in a place which involve two or more people.

A monologue
A monologue is a long dialogue a character is having with another character in a scene.

In a monologue, the character is involved in a dramatic event with another person similar to a scene. When you are working on a monologue for an audition, you should treat the monologue like a scene. **Because a monologue is a scene.**

Note:
If you are working on a play or a movie, it is recommended that you should treat each scene as one whole play or movie. This is because each scene has its own story and the logical sequence of each scene creates an entire play or an entire movie. Hence,

it is important to focus on one scene at a time and not to act the whole story of the play in one scene or one monologue.

2.3) Reading the script

It is usually observed that the common mistakes that actors make when preparing a scene or a monologue is that they start to think about the ways they will act the scene before knowing what the scene is about.

Reading a script is similar to watching a movie, where you sit back, relax, be an audience and enjoy the story.

2.4) First time reading the script

Reading the script for the first time is similar to a first date. When you are on a first date, you know nothing about how the other person will behave and how they will react to you.

Moreover, you do not know how you will feel in their presence and how the date will turn out. However, you are excited and keen to know the person and hope the whole date will turn out perfectly.

Similarly, when you are reading a scene or a monologue or a play for the first time you have to be excited and have a real desire to dive into the imaginary world of the story of the scene or the monologue or the play.

How to read a script for the first time?

1   Be in a quiet place where you will be able to give your full attention and focus to the script.
2   Read the script with a relaxed mind
3   Surrender yourself into the imaginary circumstance of the story and let the story to take you on an unknown journey.
4   Allow the words, the actions of the characters and the storyline of the scene to sink into your subconscious mind.
5   Allow yourself to be affected, emotionally, physically and mentally by everything that is happening in the story.
6   Allow **inner images*** to form and wander in your mind about each word, object and place when you are reading. (If inner images do not appear, that is fine, but if they are appearing simply allow them do not suppress them or ignore them).

*Inner images are the mental pictures that wander in your mind about all the things that you are reading.

For example: My mother ate an apple today. While reading this sentence, you have a picture of your mother and her eating an apple in your mind. Those are the inner images. Please refer to chapter 5 on further detail about inner images.

Tips:
1. **It is recommended NOT focus on feelings and emotions. Feelings and emotions come from our fulfilled and unfulfilled needs or desires, which influence our thoughts and ultimately influence our actions, speeches and behaviors. Emotions and feelings are the results of your action of your fulfilled desires or of your unfulfilled**

desires. You will feel happy if you accomplish your needs and you will feel sad if do not accomplish them.

2. You <u>NEED</u> (your desires) -- You <u>ACT</u> (you fulfill that needs) -- then You <u>FEEL</u> (your feelings and emotions. Thus, while preparing and performing a scene, you should not focus on feelings and emotions and rather focus on aspects you can control for instance; your actions, speeches, movements and obstacles.

3. While reading, it is normal to be emotional. You may either cry or laugh, allow all types of feelings and emotions to come out. However, you should NOT make the scene about these feelings and emotions.

2.5) 100th time reading the script

The word 100th time reading is being used not because you are meant to read the script 100 times. But it is an indicator that you will have to read the several times to be able to grasp the whole story of the script. You will have to keep reading the script each day until the day of your performance. **All hints on how to act the scene lies within the script itself**. Hence, the more you read your script, the better it is.

How to read the script for the 100th time:
1. Allow yourself to be affected by the story several times and go on a new different journey while reading it. This is similar to watching Titanic for the 50th time and you are still crying at the end of the movie like you do each time. You have allowed yourself to be affected by the story of the movie each time you watched it.

2. Allow more inner images come to you. In the first reading certain inner images came to you, DO NOT try to force the same inner images to reappear, but allow new inner images to form each time you read it.
3. Get in depth of the story and search for every detail about the characters and events that you might have missed or skipped before.

Checklist after reading the script for 100th time:
1. The script has become your friend and you are comfortable with it.
2. You know the story of script back and forth.
3. You can share a summarized version of the story with anyone.
4. You have been affected by the story of script mentally, physically and emotionally.
5. You learned a lesson or you identified the underlying message the playwright was conveying through the story.

Tips:
1. **Take some notes of the inner images that come to you and ideas that are aligned for performance the scene.**
2. **Research background information about author, research the meaning of the title of the play or movie and research the meaning of the name of the characters.**
3. **Allow the story to get into your DNA, and make it become a part of you. This is performed by allowing it, be patient, and trusting the process. Do not rewrite the story on another page or write long paragraphs about your understanding of the story.**

Chapter 3 - Scene analysis

Scene analysis is the process of identifying the imaginary circumstances of a scene.

So far, you have familiarized yourself with the storyline, and you have only been an audience.

In scene analysis process, we are going to start to think an actor. We are going to analyze the scene in depth so that we can gather facts about the story of the scene/play and use them as a foundation to act the scene.

In this chapter you will learn the following:
1. What are imaginary circumstances?
2. The 10 Steps to identify the imaginary circumstances
3. Ten questions to analyze any scene or play

3.1) What are Imaginary circumstances?

Imaginary circumstances are the core of a story. They are the foundation which create a scene. Without imaginary circumstances, there is no story; without a story, there is no scene; without a scene, there are no character and without characters, there are no actors to play the part.

Imaginary circumstances are everything in a play or scene or monologue. The characters, the dialogue, the costumes, the props, the relationships, the place, the needs, the actions and the obstacles. Everything arises from the imaginary circumstances.

Circumstances are the present life conditions and situations people are in because of the past they have experienced and the future they are hoping to encounter.

Your present situations, your actions, your relationships, the people you have in your life, your behaviors are the product of your past circumstances and the future you desire.

For example:
- ***Your present:*** *You are preparing for a monologue for an audition, by reading this acting book on your iPhone in your parent's living room.*
- ***Your past:*** *You cannot afford your place yet, and you own this iPhone you bought off your savings from a part-time job.*
- ***Your future****: You are hoping to get the role at the audition.*

Similarly, the scene or play you are preparing for are the present life situations of the characters.

Circumstances affect your mind (conscious and subconscious), body and soul. circumstances shape you into the person you are today. Circumstances create a character, with specific type characteristics. Human beings transform into the different circumstances they are put into.

Imaginary circumstances are the foundations that allow actors build a character by using their imagination and creativity. Imaginary circumstances are facts that you have to accept the way they are; you cannot deny or change them; otherwise, you are changing the whole story. This is because each story has its specific imaginary circumstances.

3.2) The 10 Steps to identify the imaginary circumstances

The 10 steps to identify the imaginary circumstances of a scene or monologue or play are:
1) Identify the characters
2) Identify the Dramatic event
3) Identify the Relationships
4) Identify the Time
5) Identify the Place
6) Identify the Props
7) Identify character's activities
8) Identify character's overall sensations
9) Identify the Moment before
10) Identify the Arc of the character

3.2.1) Identify the characters

Definition of a character

A character is a human being with thoughts, feelings, emotions, needs, imagination, desires, talents, flaws and relationships who is shaped into different characteristics due to the imaginary circumstances they are put into.

For example: Rose, from the movie Titanic, is a sophisticated and classy girl, who has a void inside her. The imaginary circumstances: She comes from a very wealthy family, and her mother who imposes her decisions on her each day. She is not in love with her fiancé.

Five questions to guide you to identify the characters:
1. Who are the characters?
2. Name: _____
3. Age: _____ Sex: _____ Occupation: _____
4. Key life events of the character: _____
5. Childhood/ family history: _____

Where to identify information about the characters?
1. From descriptions and information, the author says about the characters.
2. From what characters say about each other.
3. From what the characters say about themselves.
4. From the actions, behaviors and activities of the characters.

3.2.2) Identify the dramatic event

Definition of a dramatic event

An event is what is happening right now between two people that makes them be involved in a conflict. A conflict arises due to opposite needs, where one has one character and the other character has an opposite need.

Conflict is the essence of drama, and drama is what makes a scene or story compelling and interesting to watch. People come to the theatre to watch the conflicts people have to overcome while pursuing their needs. This the reason why an event is call a dramatic event.

Before identifying the dramatic event, you should understand the meanings of Needs, Obstacles and Actions.

Needs, obstacles and actions are interconnected to one another other, and they are the essence of a dramatic event.

Needs, Actions and Obstacles

Needs

A need is essential for a character's survival and is connected to the mind, body, and soul of the character. Characters will do anything to achieve their need till their last breath since their need is between a matter of life and death.

A need is fulfilled only throughout a series of actions. Characters in scenes and plays have needs that they have to fulfil. They perform a series of actions to meet those needs.

For example: You NEED a grilled cheese sandwich
- *To fulfill this need- You go to your kitchen, and you search for items to make a sandwich. You find out there is no cheese, you go to the shop, you search some cheese, you wait in the line to pay at the cash register, the cash register does not work, you*

have a little argument with the manager of the shop, you finally get your cheese, you come home you continue to make your sandwich and you finally make a grilled cheese sandwich and you eat it. And that's how the need of grilled cheese sandwich gets fulfilled.

- *You can see how many ACTIONS you have to perform in order to fulfill the need of a grilled cheese sandwich - to go, to search, to wait, to pay, to argue, to come, to make to get a grilled sandwich.*

Maslow's hierarchy of needs theory states that human being has 7 needs which are physiological needs, security needs, social needs, esteem needs, cognitive needs, aesthetic needs, self- actualization needs and transcendence needs. These needs are the primary needs of human beings. Since characters are human being, characters in scene or plays or monologues have those needs too.

Below are the list examples of human being needs' according to Maslow's hierarchy of needs theory:
1. **Physiological Needs**- I need food, I need sleep, I need sex, I need physical comfort, I need shelter.
2. **Security Needs**- I need security, I need money, I need a job, I need shelter, I need health.
3. **Social/belonging needs**- I need family, I need love, I need friends, I need affection, I need relationships.
4. **Esteem Needs**- I need respect, I need fame, I need recognition, I need success.
5. **Cognitive Needs**- I need to understand, I need meaning, I need knowledge.
6. **Aesthetic Needs**- I need to express myself, I need appreciation.

7. **Self-Actualization Needs**- I need personal growth, I need peak experiences.
8. **Transcendence Needs**- I need to help others.

Actions
Actions are verbs that characters perform to fulfil their needs.
For instance: to jump, to confront, to encourage, to question, to flirt, to challenge, to share, to investigate, to help, etc.

Obstacles
Obstacles are the barriers in the way of the characters' need.
In a scene, characters go through a journey to overcome all the obstacles that are in the way of their needs, and they perform a series of actions to overcome those obstacles.

Going back to example to fulfill the need of a grilled sandwich
To fulfill that need- you go to your kitchen, you search for items to make a sandwich. You find out there is no cheese, you go to the shop, you search some cheese, you wait in the line to pay at the cash register, the cash register does not work, you have a little argument with the manager of the shop, you finally get your cheese, you come home you continue to make your sandwich and you finally make a grilled cheese sandwich and you eat it. And that's how the need of grilled cheese sandwich got fulfilled.

Looking at this circumstance:
What are your obstacles in those circumstances?
1. No cheese,
2. the cash register does not work at the shop.

   1. **To overcome the obstacles of no cheese:** You go to the shop, and you wait in the line to pay.

2. **To overcome the cash register not working:** You argue with the manager of the shop.

A character's obstacle is usually the actions and the need of the other character.

How to identify the dramatic event?
In order to identify the dramatic event, you need to answer this question: **What is happening right now between two characters in terms of their conflict of needs?**

There are methods to guide to answer this question:
1- Identify the characters' need
2- Identify the character's actions

Method 1 - Identify the characters' need
For instance: there are two characters are character A and character B.

Questions to guide you to identify the need of the characters:
- What is the need of character A?
- What is the need of character B?

Note:
Character A's obstacle is character B's actions and need
Character B's obstacle is character A's actions and need

Method 2- Identify the characters' actions
Some scenes are complicated and hence can be difficult to identify the dramatic event through character's needs.

Therefore, you should start by analyzing the actions of the characters to determine their needs.

Questions to guide you to identify the characters' actions
1. What actions character A is doing?
2. What actions character B is doing?

Based on the above actions identified for each character, you are able to conclude the needs of each character. However, if you are unable to do so, you should answer the follow questions:
Why character A is doing those actions?
- To fulfill their need
- And the need of character A is_____

Why character B is doing those actions?
- To fulfill their need
- And the need of character B is_____

Note:
1. **When finding answers for those questions keep it simple, and specific so that you can remember them easily.**
2. **You are gathering facts from what you got by reading the scene many times. You are not inventing, creating or adding any choices at this stage.**

3.2.3) Identify the Relationship
A relationship is how two people are related to one another emotionally, physically and socially.

A relationship has a past which always affects the present imaginary circumstances of the character.

Example of types of relationships: *College friends, enemies, husband and wife, boyfriend and girlfriend, colleagues, co-workers, strangers, neighbors, flat mates, daughter and son, brothers and sisters, mother- in-law and son-in-law, cousins, elder brother and younger sister, etc.*

Each relationship has its own nature, and affects how human being the interact and behave with one another.

For example- *The way you will behave with your father, you not be similar to the way you will behave at your teacher at the school.*

Similarly, in a scene, the relationships share amongst characters, will affect how they behave and interact with one another.

Six questions to guide you to identify the relationship:
1. What relationship does character A share with character B?
2. How does character A feel about character B?
3. Does character A love character B?
4. Does character A hate character B?
5. Does character B love character A?
6. Does character B hate character A?

3.2.4) Identity The Time

The time is when the scene is taking place. It can be the time of the day, the day of the week, the month, the season and the year or era.

Time has a very significant meaning in life and it cannot be controlled by people. As time passes by, people evolve and the lifestyle of people, their behavior and their condition changes. Hence, if you have a scene which has taken place two decades ago, the way people were behaving and dressing up at that time is undoubtedly different from today. You will have to research the conditions of people at that time. It should also be noted, time is also different at different times of the day, for instance, your energy level during the day to your energy level at night are very different.

Four questions to identify the Time:
1. What time of the day the scene is taking place?
2. Which year is the scene taking place?
3. Which season of the year is the scene taking place?
4. Which era is the scene taking place?

3.2.5) Identify The Place
Definition of place
A place is a location where the dramatic event is taking place.

Each place affects you mentally, physically, and emotionally based on the history you share with the location. Hence, a place ultimately affects your thoughts, feelings, emotions, actions, and speeches. *For instance, being outdoors in a park and being in a subway are two different experiences.*

Each place is associated with particular actions and behaviors. The actions and behaviors you have in your kitchen are different to the ones you have in your bedroom.

Five question to guide you to identify the place?
1. Where is the scene taking place?
2. What is relationship of the characters with this place?

3. What are the characters behaviors in this place based on their relationship?
4. Have the characters been in this place previously?
5. How is this place affecting the characters mentally, physically and emotionally?

Examples of places: a living room, a kitchen, a park, a classroom a shop, a bedroom, a restaurant, a shop, a car, a gym, a plane, an art gallery, a boat, etc.

3.2.6) Identify Props

Definition of props

Props are the objects that the characters interact with as part their actions to fulfil their needs.

Examples of props: a book the characters reading, a mug a character is drinking coffee from, etc.

Costumes the characters are wearing can be considered as props as well.

Question to guide you to identify the prop in a scene:

What props are the characters surrounded by and interacting with?

The props can also be found through the following:

1. Descriptions of the pieces of furniture in mentioned by the author in the scene
2. The items the characters are handling and interacting with in the scene.

3.2.7) Identify Activities

Definition of activities
Activities are series of actions performed to complete a task. They are one of the actions that characters commit to fulfill their needs.

For example: to do homework, to make dinner, to clean the house, to cut the vegetables, etc.

Difference between actions and activities
Activities contain many actions that deal with handling objects- such as cooking food- you use vegetables, utensils, a stove to cook food.
However, actions in dramatic events are about the actions you are doing to the other person so that you can change the other person to make them fulfill your needs. (Please refer to chapter five later in the book for further details about actions).

Activities display the behaviors and reflect the nature and the characteristics of the character.

For example: The way you brush your teeth is different from to the way your friend brushes their teeth.
This is why you are an individual and your friend is another individual both with of you with different identities.

Note:
In some scenes, there might not be any activities the characters are doing related to fulfill their needs. However, it is advised to search for physical for physical activity which are keeping the characters occupied

For example: In the movie Titanic, there is a scene where Jack is sharpening his pencil before making a drawing of Rose. The action of sharpening his pencil is a physical activity based on his occupation and his characteristics.

3.2.8) Identify the Overall sensations
Definition of overall sensations
Overall sensations are the body sensation experienced by characters due to their imaginary circumstances. These overall sensations affect the physical body, the mind, the behaviors and the actions of the characters.

Example of overall sensations - *fatigue, drunk, sunshine, cold, snow, rain, showering, fever, drug.*

Overall sensations are things that you can feel on every part of your body (leg, face, arms, belly, eyes, ears, nose, etc.)
For example: *If you have fever, the way you will behave, speak, and move will be different to the way you are behaving when being healthy.*

Four questions to guide you to identify the overall sensations of characters in a scene:
1. What is the Moment Before the characters were involved in?
2. Which activities are the characters performing?
3. What description the author gives about the overall sensation the characters are experiencing?

3.2.9) Identify The Moment Before
Definition of the Moment Before
The Moment Before are the imaginary circumstances and the dramatic events that characters were involved in before entering the scene that you are analyzing.

The primary objective of the Moment Before is to motivate the character to initiate a scene. The Moment Before shapes the mental, physical and emotional state of the character. As a result, it contributes to the development of the thoughts, actions, behaviors and mindset of the character.

Examples of Moment Before in a given scene where is there is character A and character B:
1- Character B is already in the scene, performing physical activities on their own without the involvement of character A. Few minutes later, character A enters the scene.
Thus, the Moment Before for character B, are the actions or activities character B was doing to fulfill their need.

2- Character A is coming from outside alone and enters the scene. Thus, the Moment Before for character A is the imaginary circumstances which are the places, characters, obstacles, and dramatic event character A was involved in.

3- Character A and character B are both coming together the scene. The Moment Before for both characters will be the imaginary circumstances and dramatic event, they were involved in. Character A and B might have been involved in either the same dramatic event or in a different dramatic.

Tips to identify the Moment Before:
1. Identify the details the playwright or screenwriter mentioned about the Moment Before.
2. Identify the characters, the dramatic event, the place, the time, the arc (if the characters have /haven't fulfilled their needs), the props, the overall sensations, and the activities the characters were involved in the scene before.
3. Identifying the Moment Before is similar to finding the imaginary circumstances of the scene you are analyzing.

3.2.10) Identify the Arc of the character
Definition of Arc of the character
The Arc of a character is the journey a character goes through a scene while pursuing their need.
A scene is a journey of many ups and downs where one moment a character's need is about to be fulfilled and another moment a character's need is almost impossible to be achieved.

Three steps to identify the arc of the character:
1. Identify the mindset or intentions or motivations with which the character enter the scene in the beginning.
2. Identify the big discovery that the character makes which changes the initial mindset of the character from this point. (This is also known as the major turning point).
3. Identify the new mindset or intentions or motivations with which the character leaves the scene at the end. The new mindset or intentions or motivations will determine whether the character has / hasn't fulfilled their need.

Example to identify the arc of character A in a scene

At the beginning of the scene: Character A enters a scene with the intention to kill themselves. Few moments later, character B enters and try to convince character A not to commit suicide.
The major turning point: At a given moment in the scene, character A realizes that life is a valuable gift and they have a family.
At the end of the scene: Character A leaves the scene with the intention to not kill themselves.

The above example shows the journey character A has gone through while pursuing their need of committing suicide. At the major turning point, their need has changed which led them not filling their initial need.

3.3) Ten questions to analyze any scene or play

1- Who are the characters?
- Name: _____
- Age: _____ Sex: _____ Occupation: _____
- Key life events and of the character:

  _____

- Childhood/ family history: _____

2- How to identify the dramatic event?
What is happening right now between two characters in terms of their conflict of needs?

Method 1- Identify the characters' need
Questions to guide you to identify the need of the characters:
  1- What is the need of character A?
  2- What is the need of character B?

NOTE
character A's obstacle is character B
character B's obstacle is character A

Method 2- Identify the actions of the characters
Questions to guide you to identify the actions of the characters:
1- What actions character A is doing?
2- What actions character B is doing?

More questions to guide you to identify the need of the characters:
1. Why character A is doing those actions?
To fulfill their need
And the need of character A is_____
2. Why character B is doing those actions?
To fulfill their need
And the need of character B is_____

3- **What is the relationship the characters are sharing?**
   - How does character A feel about character B?
   - Does character A love character B?
   - Does character A hate character B?
   - Does character B love character A?
   - Does character B hate character A?

4- **What time of the day the scene is taking place?**
   - Which year is the scene taking place?
   - Which season of the year is the scene taking place?
   - Which era is the scene taking place?

5- Where is the scene taking place?

- What are relationship of the characters with this place?
- What are the characters behaviors in this place based on their relationship?
- Have the characters been in this place previously?
- How is this place affecting the characters mentally, physically and emotionally?

6- What props are the characters surrounded by and interacting with?

7-What activities are the characters involved in?

8-What is the overall sensation of the character?

- What is the Moment Before the characters were involved in?
- Which activities are the characters performing?
- What description the author gives about the overall sensation the characters are experiencing?

9-Where each character is coming from? - Their Moment before?

10-What is the arc of each character?

- Which mindset a character enters the scene with?
- Which mindset a character leaves the scene with?

Example: *You are working on a scene from the play, "A Streetcar Named Desire", and you are playing the role of Blanche.*

EUNICE [finally]: What's the matter, honey? Are you lost?
BLANCHE [with faintly hysterical humor]: They told me to take a streetcar named Desire, and then transfer to one called Cemeteries and ride six blocks and get off at--Elysian Fields!
EUNICE: That's where you are now.
BLANCHE: At Elysian Fields?
EUNICE: This here is Elysian Fields.
BLANCHE: They mustn't have understood what number I wanted.
EUNICE: What number you looking' for?
BLANCHE: Six thirty-two.
EUNICE: You don't have to look no further.
BLANCHE [uncomprehendingly]: I'm looking for my sister, Stella DuBois. I mean--Mrs. Stanley Kowalski.
EUNICE: That's the party.--You just did miss her, though.
BLANCHE: This--can this be--her home?
 EUNICE: She's got the downstairs here and I got the up.
BLANCHE: Oh. She's--out?
EUNICE: You noticed that bowling alley around the corner?
BLANCHE: I'm--not sure I did.
EUNICE: Well, that's where she's at, watching' her husband bowl. [There is a pause] You want to leave your suitcase here an' go find her?
BLANCHE: No.
NEGRO WOMAN: I'll go tell her you come.
 BLANCHE: Thanks.
NEGRO WOMAN: You welcome. [She goes out.]
 EUNICE: She wasn't expecting you?
BLANCHE: No. No, not tonight.

EUNICE: Well, why don't you just go in and make
yourself at home till they get back.
BLANCHE: How could I--do that?
EUNICE: We own this place so I can let you in.
[She gets up and opens the downstairs door. A
light goes on behind the blind, turning it light
blue. Blanche slowly follows her into the
downstairs flat. The surrounding areas dim out as
the interior is lighted.] [Two rooms can be seen,
not too clearly defined. The one first entered
is primarily a kitchen but contains a folding
bed to be used by Blanche. The room beyond this
is a bedroom. Off this room is a narrow door to a
bathroom.]
EUNICE [defensively, noticing Blanche's look]: It's
sort of messed up right now but when it's clean it's
real sweet.
 BLANCHE: Is it?
EUNICE: Uh, huh, I think so. So you're Stella's
sister?
 BLANCHE: Yes. [Wanting to get rid of her] Thanks
for letting me in.
EUNICE: Por nada, as the Mexicans say, por nada!
Stella spoke of you.
BLANCHE: Yes?
 EUNICE: I think she said you taught school.
BLANCHE: Yes.
EUNICE: And you're from Mississippi, huh?
 BLANCHE: Yes.
 EUNICE: She showed me a picture of your home-
place, the plantation.
BLANCHE: Belle Reve?
 EUNICE: A great big place with white columns.
BLANCHE: Yes...
EUNICE: A place like that must be awful hard to
keep up.

BLANCHE: If you will excuse me. I'm just about to drop.
 EUNICE: Sure, honey. Why don't you set down?
BLANCHE: What I meant was I'd like to be left alone.
 EUNICE: Aw. I'll make myself scarce, in that case.
BLANCHE: I didn't mean to be rude, but-- EUNICE: I'll drop by the bowling alley an' hustle her up. [She goes out the door.]

Let's analyze the scene by finding the imaginary circumstances of the scene by using the two methods described previously.

In the scene, there are three characters who are Eunice, Blanche, and the Negro woman.
We will focus on Eunice and Blanche as they are the main characters in the scene.

1Who are the characters? Blanche, Eunice and the Negro woman.
Name: Blanche DuBois
Age: 30 years   Sex? Female   Occupation: She was a school teacher
Key life events of the Blanche: She has a failed marriage, her husband died in car accident, she lost her school job, she lost all the money from her family and she is an alcoholic.
Childhood/ family history: She comes from a wealthy family and she is from Mississippi.

Name: *Eunice Hubbell*
Age : Not specified   Sex? Female   Occupation: Not specified

Key life events of the Eunice: She is Stella and Stanley's landlord, she is married to Steve; domestic violence is part of her daily life.
Childhood/ family history: Not specified

Name*: Negro woman*
Age : Not specified   Sex? Female   Occupation: Not specified
Key life events of the characters: Eunice's neighbor
Childhood/ family history: Not specified

What is the dramatic event?
What is happening right now between these two people/ these two characters in terms of conflict?

Method 1 - Identify the characters' need
Blanche needs shelter, but Eunice needs to help others.

Blanche's obstacle is Eunice.
Eunice's obstacle is Blanche.

Method 2- Identify the characters' actions

What actions Blanche is doing?
The actions of Blanche are to inquire, question, analyze, interrogate, and to search.

What actions Eunice is doing?
The actions of Eunice are to help, guide, escort, inform and to advise.

Why Blanche is doing those actions*?= To fulfill her need.*
And the need of Blanche is to find shelter.

Why Eunice is doing those actions?*= To fulfill her need.*

And the need of Eunice is to help others.

What relationship do the characters share?
Eunice and Blanche are strangers to each other.
Eunice is the landlord of Blanche's sister.
They have just met for the first time in this scene.

What time is this happening?
Day? Month? Year? Time of the day?
Spring summer 1947

Where this is happening?- *The place*
 French quarter in New Orleans
What are the characters' relationship history with this place?
Blanche came to this place first time; Eunice lives here; this is her neighborhood.

What props Eunice and Blanche are interacting and surrounded with?
Blanche has a small suitcase with her and a slip, on which the address of her sister is written. Eunice has no props.

Both Eunice and Blanche are outside a two story house, they enter the house, the living room and the kitchen in the scene.

What activities the characters are involved in?
They are not performing any activities.

What is the overall state of being of the characters?
Blanche came from a long journey, tiredness can be one of the overall sensations.

Where each characters are coming from?- their moment before?
The Moment Before of Blanche: She came from a long journey in order to find the house of her sister, she transferred in so many cars with her suitcase, asking people the direction to her sister's house.
Eunice was just in the house with Stella and having a conversation with Stella.

What is the arc of each character?
Which mindset Blanche enters the scene with?
Which mindset Blanche leaves the scene with?
The mindset Blanche enters the scene with = confusion / doubt, people fooled her and showed her the wrong way to her destination, Stella gave her the wrong address.

The mindset she leaves the scene with - She found her sister's house, her sister lives in a poor condition and is renting a house. She fulfilled the need of finding a shelter.

With which mindset Eunice enters the scene with?
With which mindset Eunice leaves the scene with?
Eunice enters the scene with the intention to help a stranger and Eunice leaves the scene after fulfilling her need of helping Blanche, who turns out to be her tenant's sister.

Chapter 4- Scene analysis into practice

Scene analysis into practice is the process of bringing the imaginary circumstances of the scene to YOU and bringing YOU (your mind, body and soul) to the imaginary circumstances of the scene.

In the last chapter, you have learnt the story of the scene or the play in an organized and logical way. However, only knowing the story of a movie, for example the story of the movie Titanic or the story of the film The Godfather, does not imply that you are not ready to go and act the scene. Hence, the scene analysis into practice process is important to guide you in making choices on how to act the part.

In this chapter you will learn the following:
1) Stop using the word character
2) Reframe the scene analysis questions
3) Memorization
4) Personalization and substitutions
5) Sense memory

4.1) Stop using the word character

To make the scene entirely yours, you have to remove the mindset of "MY CHARACTER", "THE CHARACTER", "SHE" or "HE". If you keep on using the word character, you will end up having another person in your mind that you are trying to become and trying to copy. Alternatively, you should start using words "I", "ME" or "MY". Using these words enable you to stimulate your impulses.

Note:
There is no character; you are the character! The character is you!
You should adopt the mindset of telling yourself, "I AM THE CHARACTER; THE CHARACTER IS ME".

For example:
"I am Rose", from the movie Titanic; "I am Blanche", from A Streetcar Named Desire; "I am Tom" from Glass Menagerie; "I am Michael" from The Godfather.

4.2) Reframe the scene analysis questions

When you are reframing the questions, which aid you to identify the imaginary circumstances of the scene, you are bringing the scene to you. You are making the scene personal to you. The imaginary circumstances of the scene are your circumstances now.

Refraining the scene analysis questions:
1. What are my circumstances?
2. Who am I?
3. "Who is my partner?

4. What is my relationship with the other person? How do I feel about them? Do I love them? Do I hate them?
5. Where am I? (My place)
6. What time of the day it is? (My time)
7. What are the activities I am doing to fulfil my needs?
8. What are my overall sensations?
9. What props I am surrounded with and using?
10. Where I came from? What brought me here? (My moment before)
11. What is my arc? Which mindset do I enter the scene with? Which mindset do I leave the scene with?
12. What is the dramatic event? - What is happening right now between me and my partner (The central conflict!)?
13. What do I need from my partner? (My need)
14. What is the need of my partner? (My obstacles)
15. What actions am I doing to achieve my need? (To overcome my obstacles)
16. What actions is my partner doing to achieve their need? (My obstacles)

4.3) Memorization

To be able to live and behave truthfully under the imaginary circumstances of the scene, it is important for you to memorize the whole scene.

You should focus your memorizing on the following three areas:
1. The circumstances of the scene or the play
2. Your lines
3. Your partner's lines

You must know your lines similar to how you know the national anthem. When asked to sing the national anthem, you unconsciously start to sing it because it is a part of you.

Thus, if you have not memorized your lines, you will spend your time on either remembering your lines or on finding your next cue, instead of experiencing and expressing the moment to moment reality happening while performing your scene or monologue.

How to memorize your lines and your partner's line
Using the word by word memorization, you can memorize any scene or monologue.

The word by word memorization:
Word 1
Word 1 word 2
Word 1 word 2 word 3
Word 1 word 2 word 3 word 4
Word 1 word 2 word 3 word 4 word n

You can refer back to the scene from the play, "A streetcar named desire", where you you are playing Blanche:
EUNICE: That's where you are now.
BLANCHE: At Elysian Fields?
EUNICE: This here is Elysian Fields.
BLANCHE: They mustn't have understood what number I wanted.
EUNICE: What number you looking' for?
BLANCHE: Six thirty-two.

Your approach of memorizing the lines for this scene would be:

that's , that's where, that's where you, that's where you are , that's where you are now, that's where you are now at, that's where you are now at Elysian, that's where you are now at Elysian fields, that's where you are now at Elysian fields this, that's where you are now at Elysian fields this here, that's where you are now at Elysian fields this here is, that's where you are now at Elysian fields this here is Elysian, that's where you are now at Elysian fields this here is Elysian fields, that's where you are now at Elysian fields this here is Elysian fields they, that's where you are now at Elysian fields this here is Elysian fields they mustn't, that's where you are now at Elysian fields this here is Elysian fields they mustn't have, that's where you are now at Elysian fields this here is Elysian fields they mustn't have understood, ...

You must keep on repeating on each word like until you reach the end of the scene.

If you have to memorize a monologue, you would follow the same approach.

Example: To memorize the monologue below:

Scotty Ryan: Listen, uh I was wondering, I don't know how to really ask you this but I was hoping you could kind of help me out with studying for the final… like, just meet up a few times cause I'm trying to pass and if I don't pass, I'm not gonna graduate. Mr. Ling told me today that everything depends on me passing the final cause my grades were bad all year long, so I know we don't know each other but I know how smart you

are in class and if anybody could help me pass I figured it would be you. I'll pay you if you want and please don't say anything to anyone about helping me cause I don't want anyone knowing I'm in this situation.
Your approach of memorizing the lines for this monologue would be:

I, I didn't, I didn't go, I didn't go to, I didn't go to the, I didn't go to the moon, I didn't go to the moon I, I didn't go the to the moon I went, I didn't go to the moon I went much, I didn't go to the moon I went much further, I didn't go to the moon I went to much farther for, I didn't go to the moon I went to much farther for time, I didn't go to the moon I went to much farther for time is, I didn't go to the moon I went to much farther for time is the, I didn't go to the moon I went to much farther for time is the longest, I didn't go to the moon I went to much farther for time is the longest distance, I didn't go to the moon I went to much farther for time is the longest distances between,…

Tips:
1. You can either use your voice fully supported from your diaphragm while doing this exercise or you can use a voice that can only be heard by you.
2. Do this exercise without giving any meaning behind what you are reading and without allowing inner images to come to you as you do it.
3. Do not lock yourself in a rhythm and a pattern. For instance, when you are reading the "Happy birthday to you" line, you will unconsciously say it a rhythm.

4. **You should remember that you are not experimenting with the scene at this stage and you are not locking yourself in any choices.**

Memorizing the imaginary circumstances of the scene:
You must memorize the ten imaginary circumstances of the scene that we identified in the previous chapter.

4.4) Personalization and Substitutions

Personalization and substitutions are two tools that will aid you to bring your imagination, creativity, personal life experiences and fantasies to the imaginary circumstances and the dramatic event of the scene.

Note:
When you are personalizing and substituting, you are searching for possible choices for the imaginary circumstances of the scene which will be useful to act the scene.

Personalization

4.4.1) Definition of personalization
Personalization is the act of expressing how you would feel, behave and what you do if you were part of the imaginary circumstances of the scene.

When personalizing, you place yourself in the imaginary circumstances of the scene and express how you would feel in those circumstances.

4.4.2) What do you personalize?

You personalize the imaginary circumstances of the scene, which are the characters (yourself and your partner) and the dramatic event, the need, the actions, the obstacles, the time, the place, the relationships, the activities, the overall sensations, the props and the Moment Before.

4.4.3) How do you personalize?

1. Ask yourself: What would I do (my actions), and how would I behave, and how would I feel if the imaginary circumstances of the scene were my circumstances?

What would I do and feel and how would I behave if:

- I was that person with those characteristics and circumstances, needs/wants/ desires?
- those relationships were my relationships?
- the dramatic events were my dramatic event (needs, actions, obstacles)?
- the places where my places?
- the activities were my activities?
- those overall sensations were my overall sensations?
- those moment before were my moment before?

2. Ask yourself - How the imaginary circumstances of the scene affect my mind, body and soul?
3. When you are asking the above question, your thoughts, feelings, emotions, and impulses will be affected by many stimuli. You then express your responses to those stimuli while performing the scene.

Note:

The answers to these questions become the possible choices that you will use while performing your scene.
You do not make up the answers to these questions intellectually. The answers will come to you organically if you allow it.

Example:
1. What would I do if I was Laura from Glass Menagerie?
Laura's circumstances: *She has a limp; she dropped out of college; and her dad has left the house forever,*
My responses to those stimuli - *I pity myself. I think I am not good enough and this is why my dad left me. I believe I will never be loved. I will spend my life hiding away from people and live life in my corner.*

2. What would I do if I was Rose from Titanic?
Rose's circumstances: *I fell in love with a guy I met a couple of weeks ago.*
My responses to those stimuli: *I want to elope with him. I will take any risk and go against my mother's will to live the life I desire.*

Note:
1. My responses to those questions match with what the characters do and feel and behave in the story. I did not force myself to think in that way when I asked myself those questions. These responses are driven by stimuli which came to me organically and made me think like the character and this is the goal of an actor.
2. The method of personalization works for most actors. However, it might not work for some actors. While using this approach, the actors are required to be themselves, and some actors have difficulties to

express their truth and they prefer to stay in an imaginary world. Personalization might not work for those actors. Thus, the substitution method should be used.

Substitution

4.4.4) Definition of substitution

Substitution is the act of replacing your personal life's experiences or imaginations / fantasies that have the same essence to the imaginary circumstances of the scene.

The purpose of substitution is to create an environment for you as an actor where you will be able to express your feelings, behaviors and actions truthfully.

4.4.5) How to know which personal experiences or fantasies would be appropriate for which scene?

1. You will sense or feel the personal experiences or fantasies from your truth, instincts, and guts.
2. The personal experiences or fantasies will affect your body, mind, and soul with lots of stimuli. These stimuli will stimulate your impulses and emotions and they will create an urge in you to go and try them in the scene.
3. The personal experiences or fantasies will keep coming to you in the forms of thoughts and images.

Tips:

1. **Keep reading your script for several times and each time you read it, allow new choices to come to you. Do not try to force or repeat same old choices.**
2. **Make the script your friend and use it as map to guide you in preparing your scene.**

4.4.6) How do you substitute?

Use :

1. "as if" my personal life experiences are the imaginary circumstances of the scene or
2. "as if" my imaginations/fantasizes are the imaginary circumstances of the scene or
3. "as if" the combination of my personal life experiences and imaginations/fantasies are the imaginary circumstances for the scene

Example of substituting my personal life experiences to the imagery circumstances of a scene or play or movie.

1. *As if the dining room of my grandmother is the dining room in the movie "Titanic"*

My personal life experience - My grandmother's dining room.
Imaginary circumstances of the scene - The place.

2. *As if my father is Tom from the play "Glass Menagerie"*
My personal life experience- My dad.
The imaginary circumstances of the scene - The character, Tom, my scene partner.

3. *As if my sister is Stella from the play "A streetcar named desire".*

My personal life experiences - My sister.
The imaginary circumstances of the scene- The other character,
Stella, my scene partner.

Substituting your imaginations / fantasies to the imaginary circumstances of the scene or the play or the movie.

4.4.7) Definition of imaginations / fantasies

Imaginations / fantasies are the product of images stored in our subconscious mind and information that we process daily into our mind. All these images and information form another reality that does not exist. When you are imagining, you visualize, and feel events or places or people that you have never experienced or met previously. You would've also know how you will feel if you will experience those events in future.

An audience expects characters to try all the possible ways in order to fulfill their needs. Imaginations have no boundaries, they are all in your mind in the forms of thoughts, images, and experiences which resonates to what Albert Einstein said below:
"Logic will get you from A to B, but imagination will take you everywhere"

Example of imaginations / fantasies
1. *I saw a cute guy on the train, and in my mind, I am imagining my wedding reception with that guy.*
2. *I am having breakfast with my pet at a restaurant.*
3. *At the age 80, I am having breakfast with my granddaughter.*
4. *I am giving my graduation speech at Harvard University.*

5. *I can also start catastrophizing by imagining what would happen if there is an earthquake and I would lose everything, my house and my belongings.*

Six tips to guide you to train your imagination:
1. Allow images, and thoughts to affect you and express your responses to those images and thoughts through movements, actions, behaviors, gestures and sounds.
2. Allow the chain of thoughts to connect to one another while you are imagining.
3. Listen, follow, and accept your guts, impulses, instincts and intuitions.
4. Do not judge or analyze or try to find a logic in your imaginations.
5. Do not force or do not be result oriented while imagining.
6. Have fun and enjoy the experience of imagining.

Two examples of substituting my imaginations or fantasies to the imagery circumstances of a scene or play or movie.
Example 1
I am playing Blanche from the play "A streetcar named desire", and I am meeting my sister, Stella, after many years. The Moment Before for the scene was me meeting with Eunice who is Stella's landlord.
My imagination: As if meeting the Queen of England is the Moment Before for my scene.
I have never met the Queen of England, but imagining meeting her, gives me a strong sense to the Moment Before for the scene. Hence, I choose to substitute the meeting with Queen of England to the meeting with Eunice as my Moment Before for the scene.

Example 2

I am playing the Rose from the movie "Titanic" and I am in a scene with Jack.

My imagination: As if SpongeBob is Jack from the movie "Titanic". SpongeBob is a cartoon character that I have never met, but SpongeBob is giving me the feeling / essence that I need for the scene. Hence, I choose to substitute Jack to SpongeBob.

Example of Substituting using the combination of my personal life experiences and imaginations / fantasies to the imaginary circumstances of a scene

I am playing Rose from the movie "Titanic", where I have chosen to substitute the boat (he place) and Jack (my scene partner).

For example - I can substitute the boat to my bedroom and Jack to a celebrity I have never met before,
My personal life experience - My bedroom
My imagination / fantasy - A celebrity I have never met before

or I can replace the boat to Buckingham Palace and Jack to my uncle.

My personal life experience - Buckingham Place
My imaginations / fantasies - My uncle

Note:
1. **When substituting the characters of the scene, you substitute the character you are playing, which is yourself and your scene partner to something from your personal life experiences or imaginations or fantasies.**

2. **Substituting yourself to your personal life experiences or imaginations is a shortcut to character work. When you are doing character work, you endow the inner, outer, and vocal characteristics of a person from your life personal life experiences or imaginations that you believe would be appropriate for the scene.**

So far, you have found choices for the scene in the forms of images that come to you from your truth, and instincts. However, those choices are only present in your mind and they are not in front of you in the form of a 3D object. Hence, in order to bring substitutions to life, in the form of a 3D object in front of you so that you can interact with them, sense memory is performed.

Note:
Sense memory is not mandatory to perform. You only do it either when you are not being affected by the thought of your substitution or when you want to go in depth for the preparation of a scene.

4.5) Sense memory

4.5.1) Definition of sense memory
Sense memory involves the use of your five senses which are sight, sound, touch, smell and taste to recreate a 3D version of the objects / places / people / events that are in your memory in front of you right now.

Example of sense memory:
When you think of your mother, a mental picture of your mother
comes to your mind. While performing sense memory, you can
recreate your mother sensorially right now, next to you. You see your
mother, you touch her, you sense how it feels to hold her hand and
you smell her favorite perfume sensorially.

4.5.2) How to recreate the substitution you chose for a scene sensorially?

The five key factors to bear in mind while performing sense memory are:

1. Use your five senses (sight, sound, touch, smell, and taste) to recreate places, people, objects, overall sensations and events sensorially.
2. Concentrate and focus on the details of the object you are recreating and exploring sensorially.
3. Keep questioning yourself about how the object you are recreating is affecting each part of your body. Your subconscious mind is where the details of the object are stored and it will give you the answers to your questions.
4. Find the triggers* in the sensory objects that will make you instantly feel as if the object, place, and people are right now, next to you.
5. Follow any impulses that you might have while performing a sense memory exercise (Example - to move, to speak, to scream).

*A trigger is a thought or inner image that stimulate your impulses.

Note:

1. Emotions / feelings such as sad / happy may come to you while exploring and recreating those objects, . You allow those thoughts, emotions, and feelings come to you. However, you do not make the objects about those feelings and emotions. That's not the goal while doing sense memory exercise.
2. The goal when recreating an object sensorially is to relive an experience with those objects, places, people and events as if they are right here next to you right now.
3. Sense memory is simply another way to exercise your imagination.

For example, let's create a place sensorially.

Let's say I want to recreate my bathroom sensorially - My bathroom includes of a bathtub, a sink, a toilet, a mirror, white tiles and a rack.

1. *I start from my actual place, where I am right now, which is my bedroom.*
2. *My sense of sight - I begin to see my bathroom and I am in the bathroom. I see my sink, my mirror, the white tiles on the walls and floor of the bathroom, my white bathtub, my toothbrush on the top of the sink all around me.*
3. *My sense of touch - (Using all my body parts) - I touch the wall of my bathroom- and sense how it feels while touching it and ask myself question what's the temperature of my the tiles, I touch the mirror and see how it feels, I touch my bathroom wall using the back of my body and ask myself how does that feel?*

75

4. *My sense of smell - I start to smell my bathroom, I smell the air freshener scent, I smell the fragrance of my shampoo.*
5. *My sense of sound - I begin to hear the noises made when I open and close the cabinet under my sink.*
6. *My sense of taste - I start to taste the hot water from my shower and my mouthwash on the sink and question myself how it is affecting me.*
7. *I have now focused and concentrated and explored all the areas of my bathroom, and I have explored how they affect every part of my body.*
8. *My triggers for my bathroom is my big square - shaped mirror - when I think about my mirror, it makes me instantly feel I am in my bathroom.*

Using the above approach, you can create any object / prop person sensorially that you consider to substitute in your scene.

An object can be anything that is lifeless such as a table, a bottle of water, a chair, a car..

Tip:
For further information regarding sense memory exercises in details, I recommend reading the book, "The Lee Strasberg Notes", by Lola Cohen.

A scene can involve any of these circumstances; the characters, place, props, activities, overall sensations, dramatic event and the moment before.

In some scenes, for instance, the one between Blanche and Eunice, there is no activity, but there are props, overall sensations, dramatic event, Moment Before and place.

In another scene, there might be an activity that the characters are involved in, but not a prop. In another scene, the character might neither use any props nor have an activity, but the characters have overall sensations, the Moment Before and a place. Thus, there can be several combinations of circumstances in a scene that you will deal with if you are substituting all the circumstances in a scene and creating them sensorially.

Lee Strasberg created an exercise called fivesome which involves the combination of overall sensations, place, object/person, activity and an **exercise monologue***that you can recreate sensorially which summaries the combinations that you will have in any scene.

***Exercise monologue** is the verbal expression of how that sensory object is affecting you. It be anything; it can be your line for the scene you are speaking or it can be the real conversation you are having with the sensory person.

Using the combination of fivesome, you can recreate any combination of circumstances of a scene sensorially. It can be a threesome which involves a place, person and event or it can be a foursome which involves a place, a person, an activity and overall sensations. You can sensorially recreate as many combinations you want which will be useful for you in a scene.

The key factors when working on a fivesome sensorially:
1. Start from a real place for example your bedroom, where you will do the sensory exercise.

2. Start by recreating your object* separately sensorially using your five senses.
3. Recreate one object (overall sensation) when you feel the overall sensations are there, recreates the place, keep recreating the four objects.
4. After recreating the four objects separately, juggle the four objects all together sensorially, while doing the exercise monologue.
5. Example: Perform a sensory activity, experience the overall sensations in a sensory place and speak out.
6. Focus on the experience you are having right now by being surrounded with the four objects while doing the exercise monologue together.
7. The goal is to relive an experience with those four objects together with the exercise monologue right now, which is the fivesome.

*object refers to overall sensation, place, Person, activity, exercise monologue.

For example:
Recreating a fivesome sensorially.
I want to recreate (1) having fever (overall sensations), (2) my childhood bedroom (place), (3) SpongeBob (the person / my imagination), (4) making toast for breakfast (my activity) and (5) speaking my own words (exercise monologue).

1. *I begin the fivesome exercise in my bedroom where I am right now.*
2. *I start by recreating the sensation of fever all over my body; I feel the heat of my body, the headache caused by the fever and*

the high temperature of fever using my 5 senses; I then ask questions about how the fever is affecting my body.

3. *Then, I go to recreate my childhood bedroom where the color of the walls is pink and where my bed is full of teddy bears.*
4. *I go recreate SpongeBob off my imagination using my senses and ask myself questions ("How does it feel to touch SpongeBob? "-He must feel like a teddy bear?", "how does SpongeBob smell?)*
5. *Recreate the activity of making toast for breakfast. I place the bread in the toaster; I wait for the toast to pop out after a few minutes; I remove the toast carefully from the machine and place it on a plate.*
6. *After having recreated all the above sensorially, now I juggle those objects sensorially, speak out my own words and live an experience with those objects.*

Using the above example, you can recreate combinations of many objects that you will use in your scene.

Let's recreate a dramatic event sensorially
1. *When creating a dramatic event sensorially, you start with the place, the characters and the conflict of needs.*
2. *I want to recreate an event where I am helping my nephew with his homework in his bedroom.*
3. *To create the dramatic event, I begin in the place where I will do the sensory exercise which is my bedroom.*
4. *I start with recreating the place, my nephew's bedroom, sensorially.*
5. *I recreate my nephew sensorially.*
6. *When I feel the place and my nephew is in the place, I start with the event (the conflict of needs) which is me trying to*

*help my nephew with his homework and he keeps messing
up his homework.*

7. *I find triggers that will give me a strong sense of the
dramatic event happening right now.*

Note:
**You do not have to do the substitution of your scene partner if
they are already giving you what requires to realize the scene
(We will come back to it in Chapter 6).**

Recap of Scene analysis into practice

1-Stop using the word character

- Make the scene yours and bring your mind, body, heart and soul to the imaginary circumstances of the scene.
- Stop using the word character: There is no character! There is only YOU. You are the character. The character is YOU.

2-Reframe the scene analysis questions

- What are my circumstances?
- Who am I?
- "Who is my partner?
- What is my relationship with the other person? How do I feel about them? Do I love them? Do I hate them?
- Where am I? (My place)
- What time of the day it is? (My time)
- What are the activities I am doing to fulfil my needs?
- What are my overall sensations?
- What props I am surrounded with and using?
- Where I came from? What brought me here? (My moment before)
- What is my arc? Which mindset do I enter the scene with? Which mindset do I leave the scene with?
- What is the dramatic event? - What is happening right now between me and my partner (The central conflict!)?
- What do I need from my partner? (My need)
- What is the need of my partner? (My obstacles)
- What actions am I doing to achieve my need? (To overcome my obstacles)

- What actions is my partner doing to achieve their need? (My obstacles)

3- Memorization
- You need to memorize the imaginary the circumstances of the scene.
- Memorize everything in the script, your lines and your scene partner's lines, using the word by word technique.

Word 1,
Word 1, word 2
Word 1 word 2 word 3
Word 1 word 2-word 3 word 4
Word 1 word 2-word 3 word 4 word 5...

4. Personalization or substitutions
Personalization - Personalization is about bring your personal touch to the scene by asking yourself. You ask yourself the following:
- How would I feel if those imaginary circumstances of the scene were my circumstances?
- How would I behave if those imaginary circumstances of the scene were my circumstances?
- What would I do if those imaginary circumstances of the scene were my circumstances?

5-Substitution
- Substitution is the act of replacing your personal life's experiences or imaginations / fantasies that have the same essence to the imaginary circumstances of the scene.

- The purpose of substitution is to create an environment for you as an actor where you will be able to express your feelings, behaviors and actions truthfully.
- You substitute by using "as if" my personal life experiences are the imaginary circumstances of the scene.
- You substitute by using "as if" my imaginations / fantasies are the imaginary circumstances of the scene.
- You substitute by using "as if" combination of my personal life experiences and my imaginations / fantasies are the imaginary circumstances of the scene.

5- Sense memory
- You use your five senses (sight, sound, touch, smell and taste) to recreate and relive places, people, objects, events, and circumstances as if they are here right now.
- Through sense memory, you can recreate anything from your personal life, fantasy, imagination or a combination of both of them.

Chapter 5- Working with the lines

Dialogues are the verbal communication people have with one another. People use words to communicate when they are not being understood through behaviors, movements, gestures and sounds.

Actions and speeches are the only two ways an audience understands what happening in a scene. The audience can only hear and see you (the actor). The dialogue reveals the circumstances to the audience. Thus, the lines in a script cannot be taken for granted and you are meant to know your lines back and forth and exercise your imagination with them. Also, the lines of the script contain words you use to communicate with your scene partner.

In this chapter you will learn the following:
1. Inner images for your lines
2. Inner images for your scene partner's lines
3. Inner monologues for your scene partner's lines.
4. Your beat changes
5. Action words / action verbs
6. Connecting the lines of the script

5.1) Inner images for your lines

5.1.1) Definition of inner images

Inner images are the pictures about the places, people, objects and events that you visualize through your mind's eyes when you are speaking, listening and reading about them.

The series of inner images that revolve in your mind, cause the audience to believe that you are talking about something personal and meaningful. This is because, those inner images are coming from your subconscious mind unconsciously in the moment.

As mentioned in chapter 2, Reading the script, you should allow inner images and feelings to come to you while reading the script. You will now allow and create inner images for your lines consciously.

Note:
At this stage, you are only experimenting and finding possible choices to act the scene.

For example: Referring back to the scene between Blanche and Eunice from the play "A Streetcar Named Desire", where you are playing the role of Blanche

EUNICE: What's the matter, honey? Are you lost?
BLANCHE: They told me to take a streetcar named Desire, and then transfer to one called Cemeteries and ride six blocks and get off at-- Elysian Fields!

EUNICE: That's where you are now.
BLANCHE: At Elysian Fields?
EUNICE: This here is Elysian Fields.

When you are finding inner images for your lines:

- *You should be able to see the streetcar named desire which you took and the car you transferred in. You should have inner images of the six blocks you just passed by.*
- *You should have inner images of Elysian Fields in your mind.*

5.1.2) How to create inner images?

By using your:

1. Mind
2. Body
3. Soul
4. The imaginary circumstances of the scene and your substitutions.

Tips: Read from your script although you have already memorized the lines.

Steps in creating the inner images through your mind, body, soul, imaginary circumstances and substitutions of the scene:

1- Read the lines, absorb the lines and give yourself a moment to be affected by the line.
2- Breathe in and breathe out while saying the lines with a fully supported voice (from your belly) or with the voice which you use in your everyday life to communicate with people.

Using your mind:

1- While saying the lines, allow images, thoughts, and feelings to come out from your subconscious mind, from your past life experiences and from your imaginations.
2- Keep repeating step above steps (1 and 2) over and over for each line without judging whether it is good or bad, or whether this is going to be helpful for the scene or not.

Using your body:
1- Re-read the lines by breathing in and out and by saying the lines. However, at this stage, think about the physicality of your body and the movements that you feel appropriate and logical while saying the lines.
2- Follow your impulses and instincts and move, sit or walk around.

Using your soul / inner self:
1- While saying the lines, allow image and thoughts to come out from your soul and from your truth. If this is the first time you are this exercise, you may experience the feeling of a current starting from the center of your body / your diaphragm and is coming up to your lung / chest, throat, and out from your mouth to the world.
2- Repeat the above over and over and be comfortable with that current like feeling when expressing your truth.

Using the imaginary circumstances of the scene and your substitutions:
1- Breathe in and out while saying the line. However, at this stage, allow the imaginary circumstances of the scene, the dramatic event and your substitutions (from your personal life or imaginations) of the of the imaginary circumstances to evoke the inner images.

2- Allow the imaginary circumstances and your substitutions to wonder in your mind while saying the lines.

Note:
1. **It is best for the inner images to be related to the imaginary circumstances of the scene. However, in some situations, they might not be, but they could be considered if they stimulate your mind, body and soul and urge you to go and act the scene.**
2. **So far, you are only at the stage of experimenting; you are exercising your imaginations and gathering a list of possible choices; you are not looking for any choices.**
3. **In a given situation where the same inner images are popping out of your mind for each time you are saying a line, this might be a strong choice; hence, do not try to change them and simply allow them to happen.**

5.2) Inner images for your scene partner's lines
You should have an inner image for every place, person, event and object that you are hearing when your scene partner is speaking.

The process for finding inner images for your scene partner's line is similar to the process of finding inner images for your own lines.

5.3) Inner monologues for your scene partner's lines

5.3.1) Definition of inner monologues

Inner monologues are the conversations you have with yourself when you are observing, listening, and hearing about the places, objects, persons and events or talking to a person.

When you are listening to someone, there is a series of dialogues that you have with yourself in your mind, which you do not speak out loud. This is your intellectual mind which is judging, analyzing and thinking about all the objects and places that you are seeing, hearing, touching, smelling and tasting.

For example:
You saw a dog in the park.
Your inner monologues: *"Aww, such a cute dog", "Where is the owner", "Why is the dog alone", "Oh, the owner is waving at me", "Shall I move close to the dog?" "Will the dog bite me?"*

5.3.2) Finding inner monologue for your scene partner's lines

In order to create inner monologue while you hear your scene partner's lines, you have to reframe their lines.

For example:
Refer back to the scene from the play "A Streetcar Named Desire, between Blanche and Eunice:
EUNICE: What's the matter, honey? Are you lost?
BLANCHE: They told me to take a streetcar named Desire, and then transfer to one called Cemeteries and ride six blocks and get off at-- Elysian Fields!
EUNICE: That's where you are now.

BLANCHE: *At Elysian Fields?*
EUNICE: *This here is Elysian Fields.*
BLANCHE: *They mustn't have understood what number I wanted.*
EUNICE: *What number you looking' for?*
BLANCHE: *Six thirty-two.*

Your partner's line: *What's the matter honey? Are you lost?*
Inner monologue: *You talking to me. Am I lost?*

Your partners line: *That's where you are now.*
Inner monologue- *That's is where I am now.*

Partner's line: *What number you looking' for?*
Inner monologue- *What number I am looking for?*

5.4) Your beat changes

5.4.1) Definition of beat changes
Beat changes are moments when there is a change in your thoughts, your conversations, topics, your actions / behaviors and movements in a scene.

In a scene, each character has their own beat changes and they arise from the imaginary circumstances of the scene.

A scene is a journey you go through to fulfill your needs by overcoming several obstacles through a series of actions. And like on any journey, you will go through lot of changes along the way.

Example 1: Referring back to the scene between Blanche and Eunice from the play "A Streetcar Named Desire", where you are playing Blanche

Finding your beat changes in this scene:

EUNICE: What's the matter, honey? Are you lost?
/////////////(**This is your beat change - after hearing the question "are you lost?" as there is a change in your thought**)
BLANCHE: They told me to take a streetcar named Desire, and then transfer to one called Cemeteries and ride six blocks and get off at--Elysian Fields!
EUNICE: That's where you are now.
BLANCHE: At Elysian Fields?
EUNICE: This here is Elysian Fields.
////////////// (**Another beat change - there is a change in your conversation topic. The whole topic became the house number Blanche is looking for instead of the place**)
BLANCHE:They mustn't have understood what number I wanted.
EUNICE:What number you looking' for?
BLANCHE: Six thirty-two.
EUNICE: You don't have to look no further
//////////(**Your beat change - there is a change in your conversation topic. Eunice told you that's the number you were looking for and now the conversation topic about Stella**)
BLANCHE:: I'm looking for my sister, Stella DuBois. I mean--Mrs. Stanley Kowalski.

EUNICE: That's the party.--You just did miss her, though.
////////(Your beat change - A change in conversation topic. Now the conversation is about Stella's home)
BLANCHE: This--can this be--her home?

Example 2:
For the same scene where you are now playing Eunice.

Finding your beat changes in this scene:

EUNICE: What's the matter, honey? Are you lost?
BLANCHE: They told me to take a streetcar named Desire, an then transfer to one called Cemeteries and ride six blocks and get off at-- Elysian Fields!
////////////////(this is your beat change - you were asking a question and now the conversation topic changed into Elysian Fields)
EUNICE: That's where you are now.
BLANCHE: At Elysian Fields?
EUNICE: This here is Elysian Fields.
BLANCHE: They mustn't have understood what number I wanted.
///////////(this is your another change - the conversation changed to the house number)
EUNICE: What number you looking' for?
BLANCHE: Six thirty-two.
EUNICE: You don't have to look no further.
BLANCHE[uncomprehendingly]: I'm looking for my sister, Stella DuBois.I mean--Mrs. Stanley Kowalski.
//////////////(this is another beat change- the conversation topic changed to Stella)

EUNICE: That's the party.--You just did miss her, though.
BLANCHE: This--can this be--her home?
EUNICE: She's got the downstairs here and I got the up.

Example 3
You are working on the monologue below where you are playing the
character, Scotty Ryan, and you need to identify your beat changes.

In Final Exam, SCOTTY RYAN works up the nerve to ask one of the
'nerds' for help studying for the final exam so he can graduate.

Scotty Ryan: Listen, uh I was wondering, I
don't know how to really ask you this but I was
hoping you could kind of help me out with
studying for the final… like, just meet up a few
times cause I'm trying to pass and if I don't
pass, I'm not gonna graduate. Mr. Ling told me
today that everything depends on me passing the
final cause my grades were bad all year long, so
I know we don't know each other but I know how
smart you are in class and if anybody could help
me pass I figured it would be you. I'll pay you
if you want and please don't say anything to
anyone about helping me cause I don't want
anyone knowing I'm in this situation.

*Scotty Ryan: Listen,///////(**change in thought**) uh I was*
*wondering, /////// (**change in thought**) I don't know how to really*
ask you this but I was hoping you could kind of help me out with
*studying for the final...//////////(**change in thought**) like, just meet*
*up a few times cause////////// (**change in conversation topic**) I'm*

trying to pass and if I don't pass, I'm not gonna graduate. //////////(
change in conversation topic) Mr. Ling told me today that
*everything depends on me passing the final cause my grades were
bad all year long, so* ////////(*change in* conversation topic) I
know we don't know each other but I know how smart you are in
class and if anybody could help me pass I figured it would be you.
////////(change in conversation topic) I'll pay you if you want
and //// ///(**change in thought)** please don't say anything to
anyone about helping me cause I don't want anyone knowing I'm in
this situation.

Note:
**While finding your beat changes, ensure to mark them on your
script as above.**

5.5) Action words / action verbs

Recap: What are action verbs and obstacles?

1. Actions verbs are verbs that characters perform to fulfill
   their needs.
2. Obstacles are anything that is in the way of the
   characters and their need. A character's obstacle is
   usually the actions and needs of the other character.

Every human being is bounded by actions on earth because life is
impossible without actions. Thus, an actor, you can only perform
actions.

Actors perform transitive action verbs to overcome their obstacles to fulfill their needs.

What are transitive action verbs?
Transitive action verbs are verbs that affect a person mentally, physically, emotionally, behaviorally and cause that person to change.

Thus, every character performs transitive action verbs to change the other character to fulfill their needs.

Example of using transitive action verbs:
Character A **comforts** *character B - Action to confront affects and changes character B*
Character B **pushes** *character C - Action to push affects and changes character C*
Character C **entertains** *character D - Action to entertain affects and changes character D*
Character E **teases** *character F - Action to tease affects and changes character F*

Beware of intransitive action verbs (!)
When you perform an intransitive action verb, the action DOES NOT affect a person mentally, physically, emotionally and behaviorally and it DOES NOT change the person.

For example:
Character E needs sex from character G - The action character E performs to change the character G are to look at, to talk to and wait for.

96

Character E **look at** *character G - Action to look at IS NOT changing character G.*

Character E **talk to** *character G - Action to talk IS NOT changing character G.*

Character E **wait for** *character G - Action to wait for IS NOT changing character G.*

Therefore; you should not consider those actions to identify the actions of the characters while analyzing a scene.

As an actor, your goal is to identify transitive actions verbs for each of your beat changes that will change your scene partner to fulfill your needs.

You can identify action verbs by asking yourself these questions:

1. What actions am I doing to my scene partner?

Why am I doing those actions? = To overcome my obstacles + to fulfill my needs

My obstacles are? =my partners needs+actions

2. What actions is my scene partner doing to me?

Why is my scene partner doing those actions? = To fulfill their needs

Note:

Your obstacles are your scene partner's needs and actions

Your scene partners obstacles are your needs and actions

How to choose the appropriate action verbs?

Actions and speeches arise from our thoughts; our thoughts come from our emotions and ego; our emotions and ego come from the desires that we need to fulfil; those desires come from our subconscious mind and soul.

Subconscious mind -- fulfilled / unfulfilled desires / needs -- emotions / feelings/ego -- thoughts-- action s/ speeches

Thus, you will know you are using the appropriate action·verb when it is coming out from the subconscious mind, needs, emotions, feelings and thoughts.

Tip:
It is recommended to have the book, "Actions, The Actors' Thesaurus" by Marina Calderone and Maggie Lloyd-Williams.
The book consists of a list of all the transitive action verbs that you can refer to while working on your scenes.

Example 1: Identifying action verbs for each of your beat changes
Referring back to the play, "A Streetcar named desire", the scene between Blanche and Eunice.
You already found your beat changes. Now, let's identify the transitive action verbs for each of those beat changes.

EUNICE:What's the matter, honey? Are you lost?
//
//
/////
BLANCHE : They told me to take a streetcar named Desire, and then transfer to one called Cemeteries and ride six blocks and get off at--Elysian Fields!
EUNICE: That's where you are now.

Your possible action verbs - To implore
///
///
////////////
BLANCHE: At Elysian Fields?
EUNICE: This here is Elysian Fields.
Your possible action verbs - To question, to
verify
///
///
////////////////// BLANCHE: They mustn't have
understood what number I wanted.
EUNICE: What number you looking' for?
BLANCHE: Six thirty-two.
EUNICE: You don't have to look no further.

Your possible action verbs -To conflict, to confront
///
///////////////////
BLANCHE:: I'm looking for my sister, Stella
DuBois. I mean--Mrs. Stanley Kowalski.
EUNICE: That's the party.--You just did miss
her, though.

Your possible action verbs - To search
///
/
BLANCHE: This--can this be--her home?
EUNICE: She's got the downstairs here and I
got the up.
BLANCHE: Oh. She's--out?

Your possible action verbs - To question, to investigate

Example 2:
To identify action verbs for a monologue:

In Final Exam, SCOTTY RYAN works up the nerve to ask one of the 'nerds' for help studying for the final exam so he can graduate.
Scotty Ryan:

(To stop, interfere, hinder) Listen, ////////
(To engage / to hold) uh I was wondering, ////////
(To lead / beg) I don't know how to really ask you this but I was hoping you could kind of help me out with studying for the final...//////////
(To test) like, just meet up a few times cause////////
(To manipulate) I'm trying to pass and if I don't pass, I'm not gonna graduate.
(To exploit) Mr. Ling told me today that everything depends on me passing the final cause my grades were bad all year long, so//////
(To praise / to compliment) I know we don't know each other but I know how smart you are in class and if anybody could help me pass, I figured it would be you.
(To bribe) I'll pay you if you want and ////////
(To beg, plead) please don't say anything to anyone about helping me because I don't want anyone knowing I'm in this situation.

Note:
Finding transitive action verbs is not a grammar competition. The action verbs can be any anything that:

1. **Resonates with you and put you in a creative state of mind**
2. **Motivates you emotionally, physically and mentally.**
3. **Stimulates your impulses to go and act those actions verbs.**
4. **Affects the other person and will change the other person.**

Use only one action verb which is simple and easy to remember, but if you cannot do so, use any word that makes sense to you.

5.6) Connecting the lines of the script

Lines arise from the circumstances of the scene. Each word, line, and sentence written by the playwright has a purpose. The sentences in a script are connected to each other. If there is no sentence one, there will never be sentence two and so on.

Thus, it is the job of an actor to connect the lines / words / phrases by staying logical to the imaginary circumstances of the scene in creative and imaginative way. Consequently, the actor will be able to create an organic flow of communication while acting the scene.

5.6.1) How do you connect each line?

You connect each line by improvising an inner monologue (a conversation with yourself), between each line by staying logical to the imaginary circumstances and dramatic event of the scene.

5.6.2) What is improvisation?

Improvisation is about coming up with words, conversations and ideas in order not to break the up the flow of conversation / life.

For example: You are on a date and you improvise; you come up with a conversation topic or even talk about weather; it might end up being the worst date of your life.

Through improvisation; speeches and actions stay alive and fresh. When you improvise, you come up with words and ideas that are in your immediate surroundings and that are coming from your mind right now. You act and react spontaneously on your impulses.

Hence, you need to improvise in a scene so that your actions appear to be spontaneous and in the moment.

Example on connecting the lines to one another with inner monologue and improvisation.
Using the scene between Blanche and Eunice from the play "A Streetcar Named Desire."

EUNICE : What's the matter, honey? Are you lost?
When you hear this line, your inner monologue- *what's the matter honey / am I lost? (the answer to that question is your next line).*
Your inner monologue you improvise to connect the line - *What's the matter honey, am i lost? Yes I think I am lost as they.....(your next line).*

BLANCHE : They told me to take a streetcar named Desire, and then transfer to one called Cemeteries and ride six blocks and get off at--Elysian Fields!
EUNICE: That's where you are now.

Your inner monologue when you hear this line - *This is where I am? And your answer to that line is your next line and here you don't have to improvise an inner monologue to connect it.*

BLANCHE:At Elysian Fields?
EUNICE: This here is Elysian Fields.

Your inner monologue when you hear this line - *This here is Elysian Fields*
Your inner monologue you improvise to connect the line - *"This is Elysian Fields, but they have sent me to the wrong number, they mustn't (your next line).*

BLANCHE: They mustn't have understood what number I wanted.

EUNICE: What number you looking' for?
Your inner monologue- *What number I am looking for? Is six...*
Your answer to that question is your next line, you don't need to improvise here

BLANCHE: Six thirty-two. I
EUNICE: You don't have to look no further.

Your inner monologue from your scene partner's line- *I don't have to look further*
Your inner monologue you improvise to connect the line - *What you mean I don't have to look further I...(your next line).*

BLANCHE :I'm looking for my sister, Stella DuBois. I mean--Mrs. Stanley Kowalski.
EUNICE: That's the party.--You just did miss her, though.

Your inner monologue when you hear this line: *that's the party, i've just missed her though*
Inner monologue you can improvise to connect the line- *that's stella, who just left his house, so....(your next line).*

BLANCHE: This--can this be--her home?
EUNICE: She's got the downstairs here and I got the up.

Note:
Do not try to memorize the inner monologues that you are improvising to connect the sentences; they will come to you in the moment and if you keep working on the scene over and over it will come to you and each time the inner monologue you are improvising can be a different one as long as it is connecting the lines together.

In order to connect the lines of a monologue, refer to the next chapter, Chapter 5.

Recap of Working with the lines

1- Inner images for your lines

1- Inner images for your scene partner's lines
- Inner images are mental pictures about the things you hear when someone is speaking.
- Find inner images using your mind, body, soul, imaginary circumstances of the scene and your substitutions.
- Find inner images for your lines and your scene partner's lines.

3- Inner monologues for your scene partner's lines.
- You have inner monologues with yourself when you hear someone speaking.
- You can form an inner monologue about your scene partner's lines by reframing the lines of your scene partner.

4- Your beat changes
- Beat changes are the changes in thoughts, conversation topics, actions and movements.
- You find a transitive action verb for each of your beat changes.

5- Action words / actions verbs
- Perform transitive action verbs to fulfill your need.
- Transitive action verbs affect your scene partner mentally, physically and emotionally and change your scene partner.

- What are the actions I am doing to my partner? = (I_____my scene partner)
- ***Example:*** *I confront my scene partner, I question my scene partner*
- And why am I doing those actions? = To overcome my obstacles + fulfill my need
- And my obstacles are? =my partners need +actions
- What actions is my partner doing to me?
- And why is my partner doing those actions? = To fulfill its need
- **Your obstacles are your partner's needs and actions.**
- **Your partner's obstacles are your needs and actions.**

6- Connecting the lines of the script
- Connect your lines to your scene partner's lines by improvising in between the lines.

Chapter 6 - Rehearsals

Rehearsal is the process of repeating, discovering and testing choices by staying logical to the imaginary circumstances of the scene.

In this chapter you will learn the following:
1. Let go of the preparations you have done so far.
2. Finding the subtext between you and your scene partner
3. Rehearsing with your scene partner
4. The First rehearsal
5. The Second rehearsal
6. The Third rehearsal
7. Rehearsing a monologue

6.1) Let go of the preparations you have done so far

In the two previous chapters, scene analysis into practice and working with the lines, you found choices using the imaginary circumstances of the scene. You brought the scene to you and you brought you (your mind, body and soul) to the script.

You have fulfilled the first part of what is called good acting, which is to act the dramatic event and the imaginary circumstances of the scene. Now, you will focus on the second part of good acting, which is to find new choices from what your scene partner is giving you in the moment, right now.

In order to be present in the moment with your scene partner, you will have to let go of all the inner images, substitutions, inner monologues and beat changes you identified.

If are unable to do so, you will not be able to be in the moment and will not be able to work off your scene partner.

Thus, it is advised to let go those preparations, be present and be alive right now with your scene partner. Later in this chapter, you will learn how to blend the choices you found in the previous two chapters and the choices you found from your scene partner.

6.2) Finding the subtext between you and your scene partner

You will learn the following in this subchapter:
1. Meeting with your scene partner
2. What is subtext between you and your scene partner?
3. How to find the subtext between you and your scene partner?
4. Finding the subtext between you and your scene partner to rehearse a monologue.

6.2.1) Meeting with your scene partner

When you meet your scene partner for the first time, you have be present with them. You should remember that they are similar to you; your scene partner is a human being with creativity, imaginations, desires, thoughts, feelings and needs.

Actors often focus on trying to give a good performance and take their scene partner for granted. The moment when you are meeting, greeting and greeting each other, is very important; you have to make use of that time and find the subtext between you and your scene partner.

6.2.2) What is the subtext between you and your scene partner?

Subtext between you and your scene partner are the unspoken conversations between the two of you which you can only sense through your mind, body and soul. You can sense how your scene partner is feeling, doing and how that is affecting you.

The unspoken conversations between you and your partner wander in your mind unconsciously when you are sensing how they are feeling and how that is affecting you. However, you do not verbalize the inner monologue out loud because it might be inappropriate to do so.

The subtext between you and your scene partner is similar to a thread that keeps you connected with your scene partner's soul. It is important to identify this connection because you will use the subtext to play off while acting a scene. Also, that subtext will ground you and will keep you present here and to be in the moment.

6.2.3) How to find the subtext between you and your scene partner?

By observing, wondering, and perceiving your scene partner

Eight questions to ask yourself while you are observing, wondering and perceiving your scene partner:
1. What is happening with them?
2. What are they doing physically and behaviorally?
3. Why are they behaving that way?
4. Are they expressing what they are experiencing? If not, why?
5. Are they listening to what you are saying right now? If not, why?
6. How do you feel about them?
7. Are they present here with you? If not, why?
8. What happened to them today?

Note:

These are not the set questions to identify the subtext between you and your scene partner. You can come up with your own questions about what you are observing, wondering and perceiving from your scene partner.

Where will you find answers to those question?
The answers to those questions will come from your soul, guts, instincts and your inner voice. You have to accept to whatever your inner voices tell you about what you are perceiving from your scene partner because this is your truth.

For example: How to find the subtext between you and your scene partner (it is an unspoken conversation with yourself).
- *"They look tired today, maybe because it's Friday, the last day of the week."*
- *"They seem sad, but they are not expressing themselves, maybe there is something personal that they do not want to share."*
- *"Oh they appear to be a nice person, I can be friends with them and work together in my future projects."*

Note:
All those unspoken conversations you perceived may have nothing to do with your scene partner. They are simply your perceptions. They are your truth and everyone's truth are different.

6.2.4) Finding the subtext between you and your scene partner to rehearse a monologue.
When you are rehearsing a monologue, especially for an audition, you usually do not have a scene partner to rehearse with at home.

However, in a monologue there is a subtext between you and your scene partner that you need to identify.

But how would you identify that subtext when you do not have anyone to rehearse with you?
It takes us back to the substitution you chose for the person you are speaking with in the scene in Chapter 4. You need to identify the subtext between you and that person (your substitution).

Five steps to guide you to identify the subtext between you and your substitution?
1. Recreate the person (your substitution) sensorially.
2. Observe, wonder and perceive the person (your substitution)
3. Ask the eight questions mentioned in this chapter under the section, "Eight questions to ask yourself while you are observing, wondering and perceiving your scene partner."
4. Let your truth give the answers to those questions.
5. You can even verbalize what you are observing and perceiving from the person (your substitution).

6.3) Rehearsing with your scene partner

In rehearsing with your scene partner you will learn the following:
1. Listening, talking and responding
2. Moment to moment acting

113

6.3.1) Listening, talking, and responding

Listening, talking and responding are the essence of life. They are the truthful way of communicating with people. They bring you in the moment where you are giving your full attention to the person you are speaking to. You are talking and responding on your impulses.

Thus, when you are rehearsing your scene with your partner, you have to bring that truthful way of communicating.

How to listen, talk and respond truthfully?
Listen:
1. Listen to the behaviors, the movements and the physicality of your scene partner with all your five senses (sight, hear, smell, taste and touch).
2. Listen to the words and sentences your scene partner are speaking.
3. Listen to what your scene partner is not expressing, but listen by sensing it from your truth.

Talk:
1. Speak your truth you are sensing about your scene partner and express what is happening between the two of you verbally using the words from the text (your lines in the scene).
2. Communicate what you perceive from your partner moment to moment.

Respond:
1. Express what you perceive from your partner through actions, movements and behaviors.

2. Respond instinctively, impulsively, truthfully, spontaneously and organically.
3. Respond to each change in actions, and behaviors of your scene partner.
4. Respond through words from your scene if you are having difficulty in understanding what is happening with your scene partner.

6.3.2) Moment to moment acting

Definition of a moment

A moment is a brief lapse of time. It is a split second, or 1 second or 2 seconds or 10 seconds or 20 seconds. It is the present tense; the moment you read this sentence is now in the past and right now it is the present and now that present is past and now is the present and now, we go in the future.

Definition of moment to moment acting

Moment to moment acting is about living the moment fully in the moment as if it will never come back again. When you are living in the moment, you are not missing anything as you are aware of each thing happening with you and in your surroundings and you are expressing that truthfully.

Moment to moment acting is like breathing. To know that you are in the moment right now and experiencing each moment fully, you need to transfer your attention to your breath. When you breathe, there is a pause between each inhalation and exhalation. In that pause, you are aware, you are present and you are experiencing life the fullest as if it will never come back again. You are connected to your inner self and simultaneously to your surroundings. You have faith in your next breath; it will come in and go out unconsciously if you allow it; you are brave enough to trust that you don't need to work on the next breath and it will simply come to you.

Similarly, in acting you have to be in the moment right now and relive an experience when you are performing (similar to breathing). You are present here, right now and you are open to everything that is happening around you. You have given your full attention to what your scene partner is doing and saying and you are living an experience with your scene partner. You have faith in yourself and you trust yourself and your talents that your next line, your inner images, your choices, your substitutions and your inner monologue will come out of you unconsciously if you allow it to happen in the moment. You are brave enough to trust that you do not need to force or to make the next choice or the next line to come because you have worked on it.

6.4) First rehearsal

The first rehearsal is about reading lines with your scene partner.

How to read lines with your scene partner?
1. Start by sitting opposite to each other by facing each other.
2. Be comfortable and put the pressure off you; and put the pressure on your scene partner.
3. Start by listening and talking truthfully to your scene partner using the lines of the script; in case you have not memorized the lines and you are reading from the script, you must not bury your eyes in the script while saying your lines to your scene partner; each time you talk to your scene partner, you must look into their eyes and then say your lines.

4. Keep searching the subtext with your scene partner with an inner monologue.
5. Look into the eyes of your scene partner and say your lines; allow your lines to comes out in the moment without trying to act a scene.
6. Allow the lines of the scene to get shaped based, on what you are observing and perceiving from your scene partner.
7. Observe how your scene partner is affecting you and allow yourself to be affected them.
8. If your scene partner is making you feel uncomfortable, express the truth you are sensing from them and channel the truth while saying your lines.

Note:
You have to start getting into the habit of reacting off what you are perceiving from your scene partner.

6.5) Second rehearsal

The second rehearsal is about finding new choices based on what your scene partner is giving you in the moment.

How to do the second rehearsal?

1. Start by being on your feet. Before the second rehearsal, you must memorize your lines fully. If you haven't done so, you are advised to hold your script with you.
2. Bring in the props you are using in the scene.
3. Follow your impulses; move and walk around while rehearsing.

4. Start rehearsing by listening, talking and responding truthfully to your scene partner in the moment.
5. Keep observing and perceiving your scene partner and find that subtext between you and your scene partner.
6. Maintain that "thread like connection" with your scene partner throughout the whole rehearsal.
7. Allow the imaginary circumstances of the scene (the dramatic event, the relationship, the props, the activities, the overall sensations and the Moment Before) to come to you and blend in what is happening between you and your scene partner.
8. Allow the choices you make (from Chapter 4 and Chapter 5) to pop up in the moment; do not force the choices to come again if they don't pop up in the moment.
9. Determine whether your scene partner has already given you what you need to fulfill the scene and you make choices based on that.
10. Allow new choices (inner images, inner monologue and transitive actions) to come to you based on what your scene partner is giving you. Keep doing so by experimenting and finding new choices.

As mentioned previously, there are two main parts in good acting:

1. *Acting the imaginary circumstance and the dramatic event of the scene.*
2. *Acting and reacting from what your scene partner is giving you in the moment.*

So far, in the previous chapters, you have only found choices based on the imaginary circumstances of the scene. After performing the second rehearsal, you have discovered that you

have to decide and act in the moment based on what your scene partner is giving you.

The five spontaneous decisions that you will have to take in the moment based on what your scene partner is giving you:
1. Your choices
2. Your obstacles
3. Your inner monologue
4. Your actions
5. Your beat changes

Your choices - While rehearsing with your scene partner, you will have to decide whether you act on the choices you made before or act on what your scene partner is giving you in the moment.

Your obstacles - While rehearsing with your scene partner, you will have to overcome the obstacles your scene partner is giving you based on the imaginary circumstances of the scene. Also, the obstacles that your partner will give you might have nothing to do with the circumstances. For instance, your scene partner might not change based on your actions; therefore, this will be your obstacles that you need to overcome in the moment.

Your inner monologues - You have to decide which the inner monologues to have with yourself based on the words spoken by your scene partner and based on what you are observing and perceiving from them. For instance, your scene partner might say the incorrect lines and you are required to have an inner monologue based on what your scene partner is saying / speaking in the moment.

Your actions - While rehearsing, you will have to decide whether to act the transitive action verbs that you chose based on the imaginary circumstances of the scene or the actions that you will have to perform based on what your scene partner is giving you. *For example, your scene partner might not be affected by the actions you are doing, you will have to change and perform different actions to change your partner.*

Your beat changes - While rehearsing, you will have to change according to the change conversation topics of the script and according to what your scene partner is doing to you in the moment.

Note:
Making choices spontaneously in the moment on stage in front of an audience keeps the performance fresh and alive. Those choices will keep on changing in the moment and they need to be made in the moment truthfully.

6.6) Third rehearsal

The third rehearsal is a about finding strong choices (inner images, inner monologue, substitutions, actions verbs and your beat changes).

1. After testing your choices and finding new choices in the previous two rehearsals from what your scene partner is giving you, in the third rehearsal, you again talk, listen, respond, maintain the connection with your scene partner and allow the imaginary circumstances to come to you in the moment

2. Repeat your strong choices (which are from your substitutions and what your scene partner has been giving you so far).
3. Test whether the choices are appropriate choices by checking if they are coming to you in the moment and making you reliving an experience on stage.

Note:
1. **So far, in the above three rehearsals, you are finding possible strong choices that you believe will work best for the scene.**
2. **Do not lock yourself in one choice; be ready to test many strong possible choices and chose them in the moment when you think it is appropriate while performing.**

6.7) Rehearsing a monologue

When you are rehearsing a monologue, you will not have a partner to rehearse with you.

When you are performing a scene in front of a group of people, the audience will see both your actions and your scene partner's action and if you don't react off to what your partner is doing, then the audience will know you are not present in the moment which is bad acting.

However, when you are rehearsing a monologue, only you can see what your substitution (your partner) is doing; and based on only what you can see the person (your substitution) is doing, you react off that in the moment.

This is why finding the subtext between you and your substitution is extremely important. **You will act off based on subtext you are observing and perceiving from your substitution.**

How to rehearsing a monologue?
1. Create the person you choose as your substitution sensorially.
2. Once you feel they are here, ask those eight questions and find the subtext between you and your substitution (you can verbalize it).
3. Keep observing and perceiving your substitution and maintain that connection with the sensorial person.
4. Listen, talk and respond to the substitution using the words of the monologue to what you are perceiving from them.
5. Allow the imaginary circumstances of the scene to come in and build on with what is going on with you and your substitution. Allow your next line to come out and shape on what you are perceiving from your scene partner.
6. Keep testing, repeating and discovering choices and act on what you perceive your substitution is doing in the moment.

Referring back to connecting lines of the script from the last chapter:
1. When you are working on a monologue, you will connect the lines based on what you perceive your substitution is doing and saying to you in the moment.
2. You make your next line come out from what your substitution is doing in the moment.
3. You keep on saying your lines as you keep on perceiving the sensorial person.

Recap of Rehearsals

1- Let go of all the preparations you have done so far

- Let go of all the preparations you have made on the scene analysis into practice and working with the dialogue so that you can discover new choices based on what your scene partner is giving to you in the moment.

2- Find the subtext between you and your scene partner

- Find the subtext between you and your scene partner, which is an inner monologue that you have with yourself about what you are observing, wondering and perceiving about your scene partner.
- While doing a monologue, you find the subtext between you and your substitution.

3- Rehearsing with your scene partner

- When rehearsing with your scene partner, adopt the listening, talking and responding way of communicating.
- Bring in the moment to moment acting while rehearsing
- Rehearse by knowing to experience everything that is happening moment to moment and express that truthfully and impulsively.

4- The first rehearsal

Reading the lines with your scene partner and let your scene partner affect you.

5- The second Rehearsal

Find choices based on what your scene partner is giving you in the moment.

The five spontaneous decisions that you will have to take in the moment based on what your scene partner is giving you:

1. Your choices
2. Your obstacles
3. Your inner monologue
4. Your actions
5. Your beat changes

6- The third rehearsal

- Test and discover strong choices based on what your sense partner is giving you in the moment and based on what you chose from your personal life experiences and imaginations / fantasies.

7- Rehearsing a monologue

- In a monologue, you make spontaneous decisions based on what your substitution (your imaginary person) is doing, which only you can sense.
- In a scene, you make decision based on what your scene partner is doing in the moment.

Chapter 7-
Performance Day

In this chapter you will learn the steps required to prepare your performance of your scene or monologue or play.

The 7 steps you can follow on your performance day are:
1. Meeting with yourself
2. Meeting with your scene partner
3. Assess the location where you are performing
4. Refer to your checklist
5. Work on your Moment Before
6. Let go of all your preparations
7. Reminders while performing

7.1) Meeting with yourself

During the performance day or the day of an audition, many unexpected events might occur. You might either feel nervous or might doubt yourself. As a result, several types of feelings might arise out of nowhere. Hence, a meeting a meeting with yourself is important.

How to have a meeting with yourself?
Ask yourself:

1. How am I feeling today?
2. What do I want and need?
3. Why am I feeling this way today?
4. What has happened to me today?

Action to follow to do while having a meeting with yourself:

1. Observe what is happening to your thoughts, feelings, and unsettled impulses. Do not try to change them or force yourself to ignore them.
2. Express your feelings and wants by verbalizing them.

For example:
I feel nervous, I feel shy, I feel sad, I feel tired, I want to go home, I want to give a great performance, I want the audience to like me.

3. Accept that those feelings, and thoughts are there.
4. Question yourself by analyzing why they are there.
5. Perform exercises from chapter 1 such as diaphragm breathing, relaxation, and affirmations.

Note:

Feelings and wants identified during the meeting with yourself, should be brought to your performance. For instance, if you are feeling tired, you should recognize this is how the character is feeling today because you are the character.

7.2) Meeting with your scene partner

The meeting with your scene partner is important because the subtext between you and your scene partner is based on what you are perceiving in the moment and it changes every moment.

It is usual for you not to meet your scene partner on the day of your performance. However, if you have the golden opportunity to do so, you have to try to find the subtext between you and your scene partner. This involves identifying what is happening between you and your scene partner today and right now.

7.3) Assess the location where you are performing

You might have already rehearsed in the place where you are going to perform, however if it is an audition, it might be your first time being in that place. In both circumstances, you should be comfortable enough to express your vulnerability and creativity freely.

If you have the opportunity to be in the place where you are going to perform follow the steps below:
1) Breathe in location/stage.
2) Accept the place.
3) Treat the place as your bedroom or house.

4) Be aware of how the place is affecting you and verbalize how it is affecting you.
5) Recreate your sensory place in the location where you are performing if you are using sensory place as part of a substitution.

7.4) Refer to your checklist

The checklist is a list of the imaginary circumstances, choices and subtext between you and your scene partner, identified through scene analysis, scene analysis in practice, working with the lines and rehearsals.

The checklist is here to keep your ideas, choices on track and organized. The answers to your checklist should be in your own words, phrases and sentences. It is recommended to them short and specific.

The checklist:

What are my circumstances?
- Who am I?
- Who is my partner?
- What is my relationship with my scene partner?
- What is the dramatic event? My need? My actions? My obstacles? My beat changes?
- Where am I?- My place?
- What time is it?
- What are my activities?
- What are my overall sensations?
- What are the props I am surrounded and interacting with?

- Where am I coming from? My moment before?
- My arc? - The mindset I entered the scene with? The mindset leaves the scene with?

What are my choices?
- My substitutions from my personal life and my fantasies - for myself, for my scene partner, for the dramatic event, for my relationship, for my place, for my props, for my activities, for my birthday overall sensations and for my moment before.
- My personalization's- my actions, my behaviors, my feelings
- My inner images for my lines.
- My inner images for my partner's lines.
- My inner monologues about my partner's lines.
- What is the subtext between me and my partner?
- What is happening on with my scene partner?
- Are they expressing what they are feeling?
- What am I perceiving from them?
- Why are they behaving the way they are behaving?

7.5) Work on your Moment before

Your Moment Before of the scene will give you the true feelings, emotions, motivation and urgency to start performing the scene. Hence, it is important for you to have a powerful sense of the Moment Before of the scene.

The Three ways to prepare your Moment Before:

1)Recall your Moment Before through:
- Inner images
- Sensory triggers

2) If you are personalizing your Moment Before, ask yourself the follow three questions:
- What will I do?
- How will I feel?
- How will I behave?

3) If you are using your personal life experiences or fantasies as a substitution for the scene:
- Recall these substitutions through images in your mind.
- Recreate the substitutions for that Moment Before sensorially.
- Relive that Moment Before and be affected by it mentally, emotionally, and physically.

7.6) Let go of all your preparations

Performing a scene is similar to go for a swim. When you go for a swim, you dive into the water with the hope to have a new experience while swimming. You do not concentrate about the exercises, and the instructions your swimming instructor gave you. You experience a new experience each time you go for a swim.

Similarly, in acting, you are advised to let go all the preparations you have made so far; the choices for the imaginary circumstances of the scene, the substitutions, the actions, the inner images, the personalization's and the sensory work.

Daring to let go of all the preparations, and trusting your imaginations and creativity, will allow you to enter the scene with the freedom of being able to do anything. Hence, you will be able to repeat and discover new choices, such as new inner images, new feelings, new experiences, and new actions, which will make your performance alive, fresh, and in the moment.

The above concept resonates to what John F Kennedy said below:
"Those who dare to fail miserably can achieve greatly"

7.7) While performing

Each performance should be treated as a rehearsal where you are:
1. Repeating and finding new choices in the moment,
2. Allowing yourself to be affected by a varied number of stimuli and,
3. Improvising by staying logical to imaginary circumstances of the scene.

Reminders while you are performing:
1. Be present with your thoughts, feelings, emotions, ideas and creativity.
2. Be aware of everything happening around you and with you.
3. Play your need.
4. Play the dramatic event and the imaginary circumstances of the scene.
5. Perform the following actions in addition to the actions you are going to perform to fulfill your need in the scene: **To be, to breathe, to be grounded, to listen, to think, to talk, to observe, to wonder, to perceive, to accept, to allow, to focus, to concentrate, to trust, to improvise, to act on your impulses, to experience, to respond and to express yourself truthfully.**

6. Maintain the soul to soul connection with your scene partner, which is the subtext between you and your scene partner throughout the whole scene.
7. Allow your lines, thoughts, actions, inner monologue, inner images and substitution to come from the imaginary circumstances of the scene and from the subtext between you and your scene partner.
8. Keep thinking in terms of the imaginary circumstances and the dramatic event of the scene.
9. Allow inner images, substitution choices, and inner monologue to come out unconsciously in the moment. If the choices do not come, focus on the next moment, and keep experiencing the moment to moment reality happening right now on stage between you and your scene partner.
10. Have an experience and express that through actions, speeches, movements and behaviors truthfully.

Final Note:

*As an actor, your job is to create a character that will serve the imaginary circumstances of the script which you have done using a **STEP BY STEP** approach and now you are **READY** to present that in front of an audience.*

Various acting definitions

Acting is acting; to act means to perform actions; you act by performing actions truthfully in a creative, imaginative, and individual way by staying logical to the imaginary circumstances of the script.

Acting is about living a dream or a nightmare under the imaginary circumstances of the script. Dreams and nightmares are imaginations; for example, dreaming of going on a date with your crush, but that remained a dream forever. With acting, you can live that dream on stage and say all the things that you imagined to tell your crush using the lines of the script under the imaginary circumstances of the script.

Acting is about being affected by a number of stimuli from everything around you and the imaginary circumstances of the scene and express your responses to those stimuli in a very creative, imaginative and unique way.

Acting is about being, living, experiencing and expressing truthfully under the imaginary circumstances of the script.

Acting is similar to having sex. Each time you have sex, it is a new experience. During sex, you have a connection with your partner that makes you understand what they want without verbalizing it. Similarly, in acting, each time you perform a scene, you must have a new experience. You are working off your scene partner and making new choices in the moment from what your scene partner is giving you.

Acting is a state of being.

Acting is an art which captures the essence of human conflicts. Human beings are filled with desires or needs or wants, and they spend their lives fulfilling those needs. Along the journey to fulfill those needs, they undergo through a lot of obstacles. Thus, actors use their imagination, creativity, intellect and themselves to create an imaginary character that will portray the obstacles human beings undergo while fulfilling their needs.

Acting is about lying truthfully under the imaginary circumstances of the scene.

Acting is a type of art, where you use yourself (your body, mind, voice, feelings, emotions, impulses and life experiences) to express your imagination and truth behind a character in an individual way.

"The foundation of acting is the reality of doing."- Sanford Meisner

" Acting is not about being someone different. It is finding the similarity in what apparently different, then finding myself in there." - Meryl Streep

" Acting is my way of investigating human nature and having fun at the same time."- Meryl Streep

"Acting isn't something you do. Instead of doing it, it occurs. If you're going to start with logic, you might as well give up. You can have conscious preparation, but you have unconscious results. "- Lee Strasberg

"The best acting is instinctive. It is not intellectual, it is not mechanical, it's instinctive." - Craig MacDonald

Acknowledgment

Thanks to my teachers: George Loros, Mauricio Bustamante, Robert Ellermann, Tim Martin Crouse, Bill Balzac, and Lorca Peress. Without their teachings and guidance during my two years at The Lee Strasberg Theatre and Film Institute, this book would've never been possible.

Ian from the East 15 School of Acting.

About The Author

Lovena Kureemun is a trained method actress. She attended The Lee Strasberg Theatre Film Institute in New York City, where she completed her Two-year Conservatory course. Lovena also attended classes and workshops at the Royal Academy of Dramatic Arts (RADA) and East 15 School of Acting. Lovena achieved a distinction for her One-year International Science and Engineering foundation program at the Queen Mary University of London.

www.lovenakureemun.com

Printed in Great Britain
by Amazon

72353924R00081